For those of you figuratively and literally attached to your latest electronic must-have, Dr. Greg Jantz has crafted a book designed to help you loosen those technological tethers. It's written as a kindred spirit, from someone who loves them as much as you do but aware of the tremendous power they have over our everyday lives. Do you want to gain control over all those gadgets that seem to control you? Put them down and pick up this book!

—Tim Clinton, EdD, LPC, LMFT
President, American Association
of Christian Counselors

W9-APH-337

#hooked

GREGORY L. JANTZ, PhD
with ANN McMURRAY

Most CHARISMA HOUSE BOOK GROUP products are available at special quantity discounts for bulk purchase for sales promotions, premiums, fund-raising, and educational needs. For details, write Charisma House Book Group, 600 Rinehart Road, Lake Mary, Florida 32746, or telephone (407) 333-0600.

#HOOKED by Gregory L. Jantz, PhD, with Ann McMurray
Published by Siloam
Charisma Media/Charisma House Book Group
600 Rinehart Road
Lake Mary, Florida 32746
www.charismahouse.com

This book or parts thereof may not be reproduced in any form, stored in a retrieval system, or transmitted in any form by any means—electronic, mechanical, photocopy, recording, or otherwise—without prior written permission of the publisher, except as provided by United States of America copyright law.

Unless otherwise noted, all Scripture quotations are from the Holy Bible, New International Version. Copyright © 1973, 1978, 1984, International Bible Society. Used by permission.

Scripture quotations marked NAS are from the New American Standard Bible. Copyright © 1960, 1962, 1963, 1968, 1971, 1972, 1973, 1975, 1977, 1995 by the Lockman Foundation. Used by permission. (www.Lockman.org)

Scripture quotations marked NKJV are from the New King James Version of the Bible. Copyright © 1979, 1980, 1982 by Thomas Nelson, Inc., publishers. Used by permission.

Copyright © 2012 by Gregory L. Jantz
All rights reserved

Cover design by Justin Evans
Design Director: Bill Johnson

Visit the author's websites at www.drgregoryjantz.com and www.aplaceofhope.com.

Library of Congress Cataloging-in-Publication Data:
Jantz, Gregory L.
  #hooked / by Gregory Jantz with Ann McMurray.
    p. cm.
  Includes bibliographical references (p.   ).
  ISBN 978-1-61638-257-5 (trade paper) -- ISBN 978-1-61638-859-1 (ebook) 1. Technology--Social aspects--Popular works. 2. Technological innovations--Social aspects--Popular works. 3. Internet addiction--Popular works. 4. Compulsive behavior--Popular works. I. McMurray, Ann. II. Title. III. Title: Hooked.
  T14.5.J346 2012
  303.48'3--dc23
                                        2011051052

This book contains the opinions and ideas of its author. It is solely for informational and educational purposes and should not be regarded as a substitute for professional treatment. The nature of your body's health condition is complex and unique. Therefore, you should consult a health professional if you have questions about your health. Neither the author nor the publisher shall be liable or responsible for any loss or damage allegedly arising from any information or suggestion in this book.

People and names in this book are composites created by the author from his experiences as a professional counselor. Names and details of their stories have been changed, and any similarity between the names and stories of individuals described in this book to individuals known to readers is purely coincidental.

While the author has made every effort to provide accurate telephone numbers and Internet addresses at the time of publication, neither the publisher nor the author assumes any responsibility for errors or for changes that occur after publication.

Contents

THIS IS THE AIR
I BREATHE

HOOK IS AN interesting word with a great work history. If it had a LinkedIn profile, it would scroll off the page and boast of contacts from all over the world in multiple human endeavors. Originally coined by the Germans to describe an angled, projecting piece of land, *hook* has found employment in boxing, fishing, golfing, rugby, the sex trade, industry, clothing, the dating scene, telephones, and even writing. When not merely describing curves and angles ("hook a left"), *hook* often describes a thing that grabs you, traps you, sticks to you, or simply fascinates you.

Apart from your money, you have something every seller, every retailer, and every manufacturer wants: attention. And every day they work hard to hook your attention, to compel your focus, to dominate your mind share. They want you hooked, addicted, and liking it. This is a book about technology. It's a celebration of the positives that technology represents and a cautionary tale about the negatives it unleashes.

Technology is powerful—drawing you in, altering your world and expectations, even defining who you are. Powerful things should be approached with caution, but many abandon wisdom when it comes to the latest upgrade or the newest technological convenience.

From Twitter to iPhones, from Facebook to YouTube, there is an endless supply of things to hook our interest, snag our wallets, and occupy our time. From smartphones to iPads, from Google Plus (Google+) to Craigslist, there is an abundance of ways to say yes to yourself and yes to technology, and there are more every day. After all, technology keeps changing and adapting to what people want and need. It's exciting and amazing and compelling. Technology is powerful—drawing you in, altering your world and expectations, even defining who you are. Powerful things should be approached with caution, but many abandon wisdom when it comes to the latest upgrade or the newest technological convenience.

If you're not careful, what you start out controlling has a way of controlling you.

There's nothing quite like the power of saying yes. The ability to say yes is heady, immediate, and satisfying. It's the feeling of having the world at your fingertips. No matter what the latest "it" app is, with the slide of that finger, the press of a button, or the click of a mouse, your options magically unfold in nearly geometric progression. But with every yes comes a consequence: when you say yes to all this technology, you attach yourself to a digital umbilical cord that can be difficult to remove—even temporarily.

If you're not careful, what you start out controlling has a way of controlling you.

We live in a world of ever-contracting technology. The 52-inch big-screen television of yesterday has telescoped down into the tiny screen of an iPod nano, fitting easily in the palm of your hand. The endlessly possible has become the eminently portable. Being accessible acquires new meaning with a smartphone in your back pocket. Staying connected becomes compulsory, and expectations take a quantum leap toward the tyrannical. *Off-line* has become a dirty word; *unplugged*, the new leprosy.

> **I ♥ iPhone**
>
> "Here's what LSD and iPhones do have in common: they make us feel divinely connected to our environments and to other people, they lift mood and bring us joy, they enrich humanity. Is that love? Maybe. But at their worst, drugs and computers can also create distance and trigger addiction, which can destroy human connection and affection."[1]

If you're not careful, what you start out controlling has a way of controlling you.

And for all of that, I admit—I love this technology. It is the air I breathe. I tweet, and you can find me on Facebook. (If you feel compelled to check that out right now, you probably ought to keep reading!) I have my Droid smartphone with me at all times. I live on my big computer (as opposed to my little Droid) hours every day. I have multiple monitors. I have multiple e-mail accounts that forward to each other so I always get my messages, which are also synched to my phone. I own a Kindle *and* an iPad. I get this. I understand the pull—the excitement and sheer fun—of so much of what will be discussed in this book. The promise and potential of all this stuff are staggering; the possibilities, functionally endless. That's why it's so easy to get swept away in a ride that takes you quickly to places where you truly don't want to go—and to places you really *do* want to go but shouldn't.

I am a true believer in harnessing the positives in technology. This book will speak enthusiastically and frankly about all the gizmos and gadgets and all the latest trends.

I'm a true believer, but I'm also a counselor and an addiction specialist, and some of what I see is deeply alarming. I want to communicate my concerns, but I also intend to present a balanced, practical approach to using technology without losing control and to help you find the "off" switch.

I am also a biblical believer, which helps me maintain balance and perspective on these matters. So along with real-life cautionary tales, I will also provide some biblical application and advice.

We are deft at keeping out tangible, understandable threats, but we often leave ourselves defenseless against other kinds of dangers, including the most dangerous threats we lock ourselves up with.

Here is what we'll explore together:

"A Locked Front Door and a Wide Open Web": It's interesting what we let into our homes and our lives. It's also interesting what we consider *dangerous* or a threat. Rarely do we know our neighbors anymore. We tend to lock up our houses, putting deadbolts on our doors and even bars on our windows. We are deft at keeping out tangible, understandable threats, but we often leave ourselves defenseless against other kinds of dangers, including the most dangerous threats we lock ourselves up with. Our computers and phones—our *connection points*—can pose more danger to us than whatever we fear lurking in the bushes. If we fail to see the danger within, we leave ourselves and those we love vulnerable.

"Multi-Taxed": Somewhere in our cultural history we bought into the fallacy that we could *have* it all. We can't. We also subscribed to the related fallacy that we could *do* it all; we believe we can multi-task—that we're actually able to do two, three, four, or more things at once. We can't. Our brain can only bring conscious focus to one thing at a time, but it's able to switch focus *very* quickly. But the number and sheer complexity of things we're asking our brains to constantly switch focus on is growing. While trying to keep up with technology, to do it all and have it all, we end up resentful, stressed out, overstimulated, and exhausted. The very things we thought were supposed to make our lives easier have turned it into a nightmare.

"This Is Your Brain on YouTube": So much of this stuff is fun. It's a blast to see dozens of "Happy Birthday!" wall posts on Facebook from people you saw yesterday to people you haven't seen since third grade. Receiving a tweet reminds you of your connection to a larger crowd. Joining in on a Groupon deal provides the thrill of associated clout. Finding the perfect YouTube video to entertain and amuse your friends at work brings social cachet. Each one is like a drug hit, a thrill; it *feels* good. It feels good for a reason. This is your brain on YouTube; your pleasure centers have been activated and neurochemicals released. There's a reason this stuff can be addictive.

"Thank You for Being a Friend": We live in world where significance is difficult to find and harder to achieve. People spend their whole lives trying to live or relive those proverbial fifteen minutes of fame. Yet most people aren't, in fact, after fame; they'd settle for just a little significance. They'd die happy just knowing their life made even a small ripple in the vast sea of humanity. This is the power of social sites like Twitter, Facebook, and Google Plus. The power of being noticed in the crowd for the last generation was captured by the phrase "You've got

Distracted Texting

If you find you really must drive somewhere, try to not let driving interfere with your busy text-messaging lifestyle! Driving while texting could lead to irrecoverable spelling errors and message failure (not to mention several thousands of dollars of property damage and potential loss of life).

In mid-2009, *Car and Driver* magazine took to the roads, cell phones in hand, to see just how dangerous text-driving is. At the Oscoda-Wurtsmith Airport in Michigan, with plenty of blacktop to tool around on, two drivers measured their reaction times while engaging in a variety of unsafe behaviors. When a light was triggered on their windshield, each driver was to bring their car to a stop as quickly as possible.

Running the test at thirty-five miles an hour, unimpaired and undistracted drivers took only half a second to brake. Adding alcohol to the task predictably delayed reaction time, but the worst reaction times were recorded while reading a text message.

Taking into account reaction times and the distance traveled before coming to a stop:
Legally drunk driving added 4 feet.
Reading an email added 36 feet.
Sending a text added *70 feet.*[2]

mail!" and it's morphed into being "friended" or "followed" for the new one. The danger, however, lies in equating "being friended" with true friendship and genuine relationship.

"Just Like Real Life": So much of the advancement of technology has to do with greater graphic sophistication. It's mind-boggling how realistic images are on the Internet and in games. But there's realism not just in how things look but also in how they *feel*. So much of our activity online from games to social networking feels real. Detached from physical reality and limitations, a digital connection allows for greater latitude in embellishment. You can truly create yourself anew via a digital interface. It's fresh, exciting, and transformational; it just isn't real.

Fast tech alters our concept of patience, endurance, and perseverance; it alters our perception of what is acceptable or not.

"Real Connection": There is an old saying, coined when people used to actually spend time outside: *the grass is always greener on the other side*. In a digital world "the other side" can be across town or literally across the world. In a digital world "greener" can pose a danger to a very special environment: your relationship with those you love. The possibility of finding comfort, solace, and consolation outside of your home, your family, and your commitments is magnified. Emotional and sexual connections can become unhinged and reattached in all the wrong places.

"Instant Download": Our perception of time, of what is instant and what is slow, has changed. Our expectations have become warped. Our culture drives the need for speed, and the need for speed drives our culture. Technology fuels this circular momentum. We demand ever-greater speed from our technology, and when delivered, our perception of fast and slow changes. Fast tech alters our concept of patience, endurance, and perseverance; it alters our perception of what is acceptable or not. The benchmarks have been moved; in fact, the benchmarks themselves are moving at a very fast pace, and our perceptions can barely keep up.

Why Swimming With Sharks Is Safer Than Surfing the Web

What are the chances you will actually die from a shark attack…ever?

Pretty slim, actually, despite the news coverage and dread the thought inspires. It turns out that there are a number of things we think are more dangerous than they actually are.

Is it possible there are also dangers closer to us than we realize?[3]

- **Heart disease**: 1 in 5
- **Cancer**: 1 in 7
- **Stroke**: 1 in 24
- **Hospital infections**: 1 in 38
- **Flu**: 1 in 63
- **Car accidents**: 1 in 84
- **Accidental poisoning**: 1 in 93
- **MRSA**: 1 in 197
- **Falls**: 1 in 218
- **Drowning**: 1 in 1,134
- **Bike accident**: 1 in 4,919
- **Air or space accident**: 1 in 5,051
- **Excessive cold**: 1 in 6,045
- **Sun or heat exposure**: 1 in 13,729
- **Lightning**: 1 in 79,746
- **Train crash**: 1 in 156,169
- **Fireworks**: 1 in 340,733
- **Shark attack**: 1 in 3,748,076

"The Angst of Off-Line": As we connect ourselves to more and more technological tethers, we become increasingly dependent upon them for our senses of peace, calm, self-worth, and security. Imagine our anxiety, then, at becoming suddenly disconnected. Previously the word *disconnect* had two common meanings—one might get disconnected from a phone call or perhaps become disconnected from reality. Now, as life revolves around technology, it's seemingly possible to become disconnected from your very life. Silence, once considered peaceful, is now apocalyptic. "What am I missing?" used to be a casual question; now it's an imperative, fraught with anxiety.

"Transfer of Power": What parent hasn't had trouble with the DVD, the cable box, the computer, or their cell phone and, rather than call a store or a faraway help desk, called their in-home technical support—their kids. Kids, teenagers in particular, know that being tech-savvy is powerful. The one with power has authority over the one who doesn't, which has flipped traditional parent-child roles and interactions. In this culture we have already surrendered an inordinate amount of power to youth (determining fashion, music, language, and sexual value), and now we're on the brink of conceding one of the last, best advantages of age: depth of experience. Technology-driven change isn't just making landlines, dial-up modems, and big-box computers obsolete; it's launching a serious attack on the relevancy of parents and adults.

The ability to control a thing lies in your capacity to abstain from it.

"Who Are You, Really?": We truly are double-minded. We long to be loved and acknowledged for "who we really are" while simultaneously fearing exposure for the very same thing. Technology should assist us in communicating who we are; it should never overshadow. When we are at peace with who we are and the source of our true identity, we are immune to the power of technology to reshape and overtake our lives.

"Find the Off Switch": The ability to control a thing lies in your capacity to abstain from it. There are times you need to log off, power down, disconnect, and untether yourself from all this stuff; it's been called a "tech detox," for lack of a better term. Detoxing from all this technology can be hard, especially when the urgency of the separation is clanging in your head and pounding in your heart. You need to learn to be OK with just you.

The best way to know how far out of balance you've gotten with technology is to simply turn it off for a while and disconnect.

"The Ultimate Filter": No matter where technology takes us, we are responsible for our actions. We are responsible for our thoughts and our motivations. The ultimate filter for whether something is good or bad for us isn't how we feel about it or how much fun it is or even how efficient it makes us. The ultimate filter for every part of our lives is God. His rules apply to everything. Don't be fooled into thinking that the Bible doesn't matter in a digital world simply because it was written thousands of years ago on papyrus and animal skins. It does matter. God is not ignorant of technology; it is His world and His creation that make it possible. He is the ultimate filter of what we do with whatever new technological gadget or program that is here today, as well as those that will invariably pop up tomorrow.

Granted, this is quite a bit of ground to cover. In order to help you do that, at the end of each chapter there will be a Connection Section where you'll be guided through a series of questions or activities to help connect you to the material, the ideas, and concepts presented, as well as to connect you to how you feel about it. I recommend that you get a journal or notebook to record your real-time thoughts and impressions as you go through each Connection Section.

For those of you who love this stuff as I do, this book is going to ask you to take an honest, hard look at what you're doing and why. You'll need to examine whether your use of technology is helping or hindering your life, your work, and your relationships with self, family, and friends. You'll need to prayerfully consider where God is invited on your digital adventure and where He's intentionally relegated to the backseat of your decisions and behavior.

Technology will continue to change, but people tend to stay the same. What we react to changes, but how we react doesn't.

For any who are skeptical and suspicious of technology who may have picked up this book in hopes of depositing it under the nose of a family member or friend while saying, "Here, read this! I told you so!"...you may be a little disappointed. Technology is not only the air I breathe, but it's also everywhere around us. It's how the world communicates and interacts, for better or for worse. More importantly, it's especially the way the next generation communicates and interacts. Wishing it didn't exist and longing for the days when being away from home meant being away from the phone is just that—wishful thinking. We may be less than two score years into this brave new world, but the cultural landscape has been permanently altered. If that skeptic is you, I encourage you to read this book anyway. Hopefully you'll gain some insight and also pass it along to someone who truly needs it.

In some ways this book is a bit of déjà vu. Over a decade ago I wrote another book about technology, written when the term *Internet* found its way into public discourse. That book looked at the potential of this new medium, then known as the *World Wide Web*, lauding its positives while warning about its negatives. In researching this book, I was surprised at how similar the struggles are from then to now: back then it was getting up at two in the morning to check e-mail; now it's Facebook. Back then it was spending hours and hours surfing the Web; now it's sexting. Back then it was chatting; now it's tweeting.

Technology will continue to change, but people tend to stay the same. *What* we react to changes, but *how* we react doesn't. Each of us is bound by human nature. This book is not about helping you gain control over the latest technological gadgets and fads; rather, it's about helping you gain control over yourself. Then, whatever technology comes your way, you'll be able to use it, or not, with yourself in control. So, while this book is going to describe what's latest on the scene, the bulk of discovery is going to come from something that's been around a little longer—you.

I said at the beginning of this introduction, "This is a book about technology. It's a celebration of the positives that technology represents and a cautionary tale about the negatives it unleashes." Perhaps I need to be a little clearer at the end of this introduction: the positives and negatives unleashed are not *from* technology; they are *through* technology. The positives and negatives technology unleashes are ultimately personal; they come from inside you. The connection that makes the most difference where all this technology is concerned is the one you have with yourself.

Chapter 1

A LOCKED FRONT DOOR AND A WIDE OPEN WEB

I N EARLY 2011 design student Alex Trimpe uploaded an "info-graphic" video to YouTube called "The World Is Obsessed With Facebook." It's a visually engaging display of interesting Facebook factoids, the collection of which is credited to online schools.org. The music is catchy and upbeat, providing a light and carefree background to some staggering statistics:[1]

- There are 500 million Facebook users worldwide, or 1 out of every 13 people alive.

- Forty-eight percent of eighteen- to thirty-four-year-olds check Facebook upon waking.

- Those ages thirty-five and up constitute over 30 percent of Facebook users.

- The percentage of the US Web audience on Facebook is 71.2 percent.

- Fifty-seven percent of people say they talk more online than they do in real life.

- Forty-eight percent of young people say they get their news on Facebook.

- Over a single New Year's weekend 750 million photos were posted on Facebook.

- Every twenty minutes on Facebook the following occurs:

  - There are 1 million shared links.

  - Over 1.3 million photos are tagged.

  - Almost 1.5 event invites are sent.

  - Over 1.8 million people update their status.

  - Almost 2 million people accept a friend request.

  - Over 2.7 million photos are uploaded, with equivalent messages sent.

  - Over 1.5 million wall posts are added.

If you think back over the last five years, how much of your life was devoted to online activities? How much of your real life has been gobbled up or googled up in your net life?

Appropriately, at the end of the video viewers have an opportunity to "share this on Facebook."

Go onto any search engine and enter a word, like *cheese*. On Google (as of this writing) you can browse through approximately 319 million pages, if you wanted and had enough time. Pick any word, choose any subject, and there are more options for you to choose from than there are hours, minutes, or seconds in the day. If you were interested (really, truly interested) in cheese and took just thirty seconds to peruse every page listed on Google, it would take you over 303 years to view them all—with no stopping for food, drink, or sleep. Of course, "cheese" is a fairly undefined search, so enter *parmesan cheese* (without quotes), and you could handle that result set in a little over ten years. Now, you might counter that this is a ridiculous example—no sane person would waste ten years of their life surfing the Web for parmesan cheese. I'll grant you, maybe cheese isn't actually that compelling, but have you considered how much time you actually do spend online in

Google, the Hungry Web Spider

When Google Plus was barely one hundred days old with 40 million users already signed up, Google's chief business officer Nikesh Arora denied that 800-million-member Facebook was any kind of rival. Google Plus "is not a social network," he said. Rather, "It is a platform which allows us to bring *social elements into all the services and products that we offer*" (emphasis added). Arora added that Web users would simply have to get used to surrendering more and more personal information about themselves and their preferences in order to take advantage of online services that are socially wired.

As one conference delegate put it, "Google+ is just a big spider," but one that is spinning a vast web of products, services, profiles, and personal data.[2] Will it have yours too?

a day, in a week, in a month, or throughout the year? Is that amount less than it used to be or more? If you think back over the last five years, how much of your life was devoted to online activities? How much of your real life has been gobbled up or googled up in your net life?

According to a social media page on Facebook, people spend over 700 billion minutes per month on Facebook.[3] Statistics from Facebook show 50 percent of their active users logging on during any given day.[4] Seven hundred billion minutes per month. That means, if I did my math correctly, every month Facebook users consume over one million years of life.[5] Granted, at this time Facebook claims around 800 million active users[6] to spread out those 700 billion minutes. Still, that means that every Facebook user, on average, spends a full twenty-four-hour day logged on *each month*. Added up like that, it may seem like a lot. But that's what you get when you *only* spend one hour every day surfing Facebook.

No wonder television viewership is dropping.

Millions and millions of pages, pictures, videos, and posts—all through the computer that hunkers on your desk, the tablet you lean back with on the couch, or the phone you keep tethered on you at all times. Instantly, anytime, anywhere, you can join with hundreds of millions of users in the digital community. It's a world of geometric possibilities and vast potential, so is it naïve to wonder whether those vast possibilities are all positive or whether all that potential is beneficial?

Technology moves so fast that stopping to take a second look means being left behind.

Dealing with something this compelling, this transformational, this far-reaching calls for at least a small bit of caution.

Caution and *technology* are two words not often used in polite conversation. Caution is all about holding up, slowing down, taking a wait-and-see attitude. Technology, though, is all about full speed ahead, ramping up, taking an I-can't-wait-to-see-what's-next attitude. Caution involves taking into account what's gone on before. Technology has a way of trashing what's gone on before, as landfills and recycling centers can attest. Caution acknowledges you might not be right at first, so take a second look. Technology moves so fast that stopping to take a second look means being left behind.

There are many people who do not want to be left behind. I admit; I'm one of them. I may not be the first one on my block to have the latest gadget, but I'm close. It is so easy for me to identify the wow factor, the fun factor, in technology. It takes a little longer for the caution part of my brain to catch up. Part of me wants to argue, "What's the problem? All of this stuff is great, right?"

It wasn't so great for a forty-three-year-old Tacoma man, James Sanders: he's dead now. Sanders merely decided to advertise a diamond ring for sale on Craigslist. According to court documents, when twenty-two-year-old Kiyoshi Higashi arrived to look at the ring, he brought three friends with him. They forced their way into the Sanders' home, where they bound Sanders and his family with plastic ties, then shot Mr. Sanders to death in front of his wife and children.[7]

It wasn't so great for Pat Blucher. She's not dead, but she's missing a significant amount of money. She thought she was sending it to her granddaughter who called from Canada with a story of being arrested and needing bail money. There was only one problem: the person on the phone was not Pat's granddaughter but an imposter. Using personal information gleaned from Facebook pages, the woman on the phone seeded her story with enough family details to convince Pat to send thousands of dollars to Canada.[8]

It wasn't so great for Janice Robinson. She started talking to Mark Johnson over Facebook, thinking he might be someone she knew. He wasn't, but his story and pictures were still enough to pull at Janice's heartstrings, so she kept communicating. Mark told Janice he was a lonely soldier looking for love—love and...oh, by the way, money. Janice didn't start digging into her wallet; she started digging into the Facebook information. On one of the pictures of Mark Johnson she found the name *James Hursey*. Hursey was indeed a soldier, an Army sergeant, who had returned from Iraq with a back injury. He was rather surprised to find his images being used by someone else in a scam to defraud women over the Internet.[9]

It didn't turn out so great for Megan Meier—although at first it seemed otherwise. Megan was able to connect with a teenage boy she liked over MySpace. But Megan was devastated when the boy dumped her, saying the world would be better off without her. In despair, Megan ended her life at age thirteen over a boy she was in love with but had never met. A boy who wasn't even real, whose MySpace profile had been created as a hoax by three people—a teenage girl acquaintance, her mother, and the mother's business associate. That mother, Lori Drew, was charged with creating a fake account on MySpace, but the charges were later dropped because of the vagueness of the law.[10]

There is a saying that goes, "All that glitters is not gold." Technology, especially new technology, glitters. It is polished and displayed in the most favorable light by those who want to sell it and viewed positively by those who want to acquire it. However, caution dictates that while it glitters it *may* be gold, but a wise person should look closely at it first to be sure.

> ## We tend to lock up our houses, deadbolt on the doors, and bar the windows. We keep out tangible, understandable threats but often leave ourselves wide open to other kinds of dangers.

UNLIMITED ACCESS

It's interesting what we let into our homes and our lives and what we keep out. It's interesting what we consider *dangerous* or a threat. Rarely do we know our neighbors anymore. We don't let our kids walk home by themselves from school or play unsupervised in our neighborhoods. We tend to lock up our houses, deadbolt on the doors, and bar the windows. We keep out tangible, understandable threats but often leave ourselves wide open to other kinds of dangers.

Technology is a connection point. It is the way we reach out and connect—to information, to services, to other people. It is also a way for other people to connect to us, whether we desire it or not. Technology grants us access to a vast array of information, but it also allows others access to our private lives and personal details. It bypasses our locked doors and windows, our security systems and guard dogs, because we allow it into our most intimate spaces. Our computers, our phones, and our connection points can pose more danger and be more problematic to us than anything we imagine lurking in the bushes outside our homes. If we fail to see the risks, we leave ourselves and those we love wide open. Skeptical? Again, just ask Pat Blucher, Janice Robinson, James Hursey, or the families of James Sanders and Megan Meiers.

When you put yourself out there on the Internet, you're

establishing connection; you're opening up an access point. Every connection is a two-way conversation, whether you mean it to be or not. For example, you may simply use Google to search for something interesting, but in the process Google has recorded your interests, where you've been, and what you like. You think your information is private because you didn't log on and provide a user name, but Google records the Internet address you used, and all the previous addresses too. It records your location, the kind of device you're using, your favorite browser, and more. And if you've *ever* signed in to Google, all of that information can be correlated. When you use the Internet to discover things, you invariably reveal more than you know—it's unavoidable. Have you ever noticed when you go online that many of the ads sprinkled around websites are tailored to your location, gender, age, previously visited websites, and even searches you've performed? If you use an online webmail service like Gmail, the ads are even tailored to the contents of the messages you read. This isn't coincidental; you're being targeted, and you provided the information, the ammunition, yourself.

Today it's automatically targeted advertising, but what will it be tomorrow? I ran across an interesting statement from Julian Assange, the founder of Wikileaks, from a couple of years ago. While speaking to students at Cambridge University, he said, "So while the Internet has in some ways an ability to let us know to an unprecedented level what government is doing…it is also the greatest spying machine the world has ever seen."[11] Technology results in us both knowing and being known.

Every connection is a two-way conversation, whether you mean it to be or not.

I don't mean to sound like a neo-Luddite or a conspiracy theorist, but this knowledge does lead me to approach what I do on the Internet with a certain amount of care. Technology allows us to personalize our world to an amazing degree, to tailor what we see, hear, and say. This customization gives us the illusion of total control and makes it ever more difficult to see and admit how technology could be controlling and changing us.

LOVE AFFAIR

Getting a novel gadget or using technology in a new way is much like entering into a new relationship. I remember when I got my first computer: I was in love. I remember when I first discovered the Internet: I was in love. Same thing when I started e-mailing: love at first byte! At first I couldn't get enough of any of it. These technologies were intriguing, compelling, and astonishing. Of course, after time, I found myself spending far too much time on the computer, and a couple of times I wound up somewhere on the Internet I had no business being. I used to be thrilled to get a dozen e-mails; now I process hundreds daily.

In the beginning I envision how much time these technologies will save me. Remarkably, there is still not enough time at the end of my day. At first all of these new innovations are fun and exciting. But over time they've become a little less innovative and a little more intrusive. Where once I couldn't wait to log on to Facebook, now I do so with a bit of sigh at times.

All this technology delivers on some of their promises, but not all, and occasionally I find myself looking for my next "relationship." I've come to realize I have a tendency to respond to new technology as the ancient Israelites did with manna in the wilderness: at first, it's a godsend, but before long I find myself complaining and looking around for something new.

A Great Cloud of Witnesses

Various websites track different pieces of information about you while you're surfing the Web. Your friendly neighborhood social network may know more about you than you realize.

In interviews with an engineering director, an engineering manager, and three corporate spokesmen, *USA Today* discovered how Facebook was tracking users in late 2011.

If you are logged in and using a Facebook account, you get two kinds of "cookies," browser-based tracking files: one is a "session cookie," and one is a "browser cookie." If you don't log in and don't have an account, you only get a browser cookie.

Then, whenever you visit a third-party page that uses the Facebook Like button (or some other Facebook plug-in such as for commenting), Facebook logs the date and time, the URL you're viewing, your IP address, and various computer and browser characteristics (screen resolution, operating system, browser version, and so on). If you've previously logged into Facebook, this data is associated with your profile information, including your name, e-mail address, your friends, and anything else you've disclosed to the social media network.

But even if you've never logged into Facebook and don't have a browser cookie associated with your profile, you still get tagged with a unique ID.

According to the article, Facebook's engineering director, Arturo Bejar, acknowledged that "Facebook could learn where specific members go on the Web when they are logged off by matching the unique PC and browser characteristics logged by both the session cookie and the browser cookie."

Facebook may not do this kind of tracking and correlation itself (yet), but online banner ad suppliers do. After all, "More data means better targeting, which means more revenue."[12]

Exceptional Life

Which brings me to another connection point of technology I'd like you to consider: technology connects you to others, good or bad, but it also connects you to yourself, good or bad. It's amazing what you learn about yourself when you think you're in control, when you're sure you're in charge. As I often warn, "Those who make the rules break the rules." Technology gives you the impression you're making your own rules. So when under the illusion of that control, it's interesting to see which of your personal rules you're willing to break, where you're willing to compromise, and what areas of your character produce the greatest amount of excuses and rationalizations.

Technology has a way of tempting me to make exceptions where my personal rules apply. For example, I try to obey traffic laws when driving, but I underwent an almost militant rebellion when the state of Washington outlawed using cell phones while driving. Up to that point I had become quite accustomed and comfortable paying marginal attention to the road and, sometimes, intense attention to my phone conversations—even when my family was in the car. It took me quite a while (and a hands-free Bluetooth) to quell my resentment at being told I was not competent to both drive and hold my cell phone at the same time.

Technology connects you to others, good or bad, but it also connects you to yourself, good or bad.

I know there is research out there that shows it's not holding the cell phone that's the problem; it's the conversation itself that's distracting.[13] Still, I anticipate being less than grateful when the ban expands to driving while using a cell phone at all. I rely on my drive time to catch up on voice mail and make necessary phone calls. I *like* this technology and want to continue using it. Like everybody else, I think of myself as exceptional: I'm not *impaired* just because I'm loudly discussing with my wife the actual location of my kids' soccer game while driving in distracted circles through strange neighborhoods. I don't appreciate being told not to do something I consider myself capable of doing well.

Technology, you see, has a way of making me feel even more in control, more in charge, and more capable than I actually am.

Before I had kids, I remarked that I wasn't going to become one of those parents who went out and bought the latest and the greatest gadget for their kids. When I made that rule, I was childless and Gameboys, Wiis, Kindles, PlayStations, and Xboxes weren't even on the drawing boards yet. When I made that rule, I fully intended to keep it.

Recently I appeared on a local morning television show. The topic was how we've become so tied to all of these gadgets. I took my two boys along with me because I thought it would be fun for them to visit the studio and watch their dad on TV. I also brought along an array of our family devices. With chagrin, then, I had to admit to the host, both of us looking down at a table full of stuff, that I'd made mistakes where technology was concerned. Even though it was difficult admitting those mistakes, imagine my surprise when my sons joined me on live television to talk about them! I realized that because I'm so personally enamored with technology, I'd made an exception to my own rule and ultimately bought my kids more games and gadgets than they ever needed. Because I like the gadgets myself, I allowed my boys to plug into them and disconnect from people too long and too often.

These are some personally embarrassing, though benign, examples of how technology lured me into making exceptions. As a professional counselor I've seen less benign and more devastating examples of how technology has lured others into doing and viewing and saying things they later regretted. I've seen technology propel people into situations they feel powerless to exit. I've seen the use of technology reveal aspects of character, integrity, and personal weakness that both shocked and shamed the one exposed. I've seen great surprise over the power these things can have in personal lives and choices. Over and over again I've heard people confess they started some technology-empowered behavior believing they had control. Then they come to my office after realizing they were being controlled instead.

Technology has a way of making me feel even more in control, more in charge, and more capable than I actually am.

Caution is warranted. Technology is powerful, not only in what it can provide but also in what it can elicit. It enables connection. Many of those connections are wonderful, fun, and even useful, but some connections are problematic. You need to be alert to the problems others can bring into your life. You need to be aware of the problems you can bring upon yourself and your relationships. You need to be honest with yourself about how often, how much, and why you're tethered to your technology and whether that's a positive or a negative in your life.

=== **CONNECTION SECTION** ===

Just as I had to do for that television show, I want you to mentally lay all your stuff out on the table. I have designed a chart below to help you with this process. You can write in this book, or you can use your journal or a notebook. Under the chart are the instructions to follow to complete this exercise.

MY PERSONAL TECHNOLOGY USE				
+ or -	Activity	Dollar Amount	Time per Day	Time per Week
	1.			
	2.			
	3.			
	4.			
	5.			
	6.			
	7.			
	8.			
	9.			
	10.			

Write down all the ways you interact with technology during your day, from cell phones to smartphones, from computers to laptops, from game consoles to Internet access: list them all.

Next, I'd like you to put down a dollar figure for each. How much has each one cost you? After you've made your best guess on each, run a total. What is your reaction to the total? Is it less than you thought? More? Remember, with finite resources, every dollar you spend on this technology generally means money not saved or spent somewhere else.

You've calculated money spent, but how about time spent? How much time per day do you spend with these things? How much time per week? Based on your amount, calculate how much time you spend per month and per year. Again, what are your reactions to these amounts? Are you surprised? Time and money can be very similar in that both are finite. Time spent on these activities means time removed from others. (Even if you are required to use technology in your workplace and career, think of the time-wasting activities that weren't directly related to getting work done. You'd be surprised how much time "at work" is frittered away on nonproductive online activities.)

As you think of your life and how you're using your time now, what have you reduced or eliminated in order to make room for your love of technology? For example, if you spend more time texting friends, do you spend less time actually talking to them, actually seeing them in person? If you spend more time online than you used to, does that mean you spend less time watching television, less time outside? What about time with your family?

Now, return to your list. Next to each activity or item listed, I want you to think whether it is a positive or a negative in your life. Write either a "+" or a "-" next to each. I'm going to assume that most of the things on your list started out positive, so if one has switched to a negative, try to determine when it happened.

People who have walked through this exercise with me have been surprised at how much time from their lives is consumed by some sort of technology. One friend knew she was spending a lot of time on Facebook but wasn't sure how much, so she decided to track it for a week. When her log revealed that "Facebooking" was equivalent to a part-time job, she realized things had gotten out of hand. Concrete numbers have a way of dispelling vague impressions and delusions.

If you've just buzzed through the preceding paragraphs without any real intention of doing the exercises, I'd like you to reconsider. Please stop and take time to catalog your use and its impact. Excuses and exceptions have a way of obscuring truth; this exercise can produce a great degree of clarity. Clarity brings truth into sharp focus.

When her log revealed that "Facebooking" was equivalent to a part-time job, she realized things had gotten out of hand.

When dealing with powerful things, seeing clearly is extremely important.

Chapter 2

MULTI-TAXED

YOU'VE PROBABLY HEARD the joke about people who can't walk and chew gum at the same time. That joke has a modern update: at the Berkshire Mall in Reading, Pennsylvania, a woman was texting and walking at the same time. So intent was she on her phone she failed to notice the large decorative fountain in her path. *Splash!* Without hesitation in she went, caught on the mall's surveillance cameras. Video of her plunge, from different angles, soon found its way onto YouTube, then multiplied across more video sharing sites. The plunge briefly captured the cyber-psyche as people viewed her self-absorbed mishap millions of times. Then it went off-line as news outlets talked about it, showing her headlong plunge into the fountain and her emergence completely drenched, over and over again. The woman subsequently hired an attorney because of the "humiliation" of having her image become the latest viral Internet joke.[1]

Perhaps the reason so many found her predicament compelling was not simply because it was funny, but because they could completely relate. I know I could. Most of us don't take a header into a mall fountain, but plenty of us have been less than successful trying to do two things at once. And that's just two things. Consider our success rate when trying to juggle three, four, or more things. It's called multitasking, and many of us rely on this skill to get through our day. With so many things demanding our attention at any given moment, it's easy to get snared in the frenzy. Perversely, the more labor-saving devices we employ, the more we have to do and the less time we have.

Maybe you grew up in a household with a single phone. When that thing rang, you had to drop whatever you were doing to answer it. It might be important; you might be missing something you needed to know. "Grab the phone!" was a verbal imperative, delivered with great intensity. The phone trumped nearly everything; it got your immediate attention. It still gets mine, and I have *three* of them; the one at my house, my cell phone, and the one at my work that has eight lines. I live in a world of ringing phones. No matter how pleasant I try to make the ring, it still produces an echo of that frantic "grab the phone" imperative.

The more labor-saving devices we employ, the more we have to do and the less time we have.

Everywhere I go, I am accessible by phone. I have given it access because it is supposed to make my life easier. In some ways it has. If I have a thought, want, or need, I have the ability to pick up my phone and access others to address my thought, want, or need immediately. But the double-edged sword cuts both ways: other people also have the ability to instantly access me to address their own thoughts, wants, or needs.

It's a double-edged sword in another way as well. Before, when phones were limited to landlines, if I wanted to call someone, I had to wait while I relocated myself to find a phone. If the inconvenience of finding a phone wasn't enough to put me off, by the time I found the phone I might have decided I actually didn't need to make that call after all. Now, time and inconvenience are no filter: I can make that call the moment I think of it. No waiting, no contemplating, just doing. If I have an impulse, I can act on it.

This impulsivity isn't restricted to phones either. The more gadgets and gizmos I have around me, the more opportunity I have to act on even more impulses.

Two Things at Once

The problem with acting on and adding to my impulses is that I'm generally already trying to do something else. After all, it's much quicker to *think* of what to do than it is to actually accomplish it. But technology has tricked me into thinking the gap between thinking and accomplishing has narrowed. In many ways it has, but not as much as promised. With technology, I keep telling myself, "This won't take very long," or "This will take only a minute." And before I know it, I've acted on my various impulses and find myself juggling multiple things at once.

You would think I'd know better. I used to consider myself a whiz at multitasking; at least, it seemed that way. I could talk on the phone, check my e-mail, sign a document, answer a question, and eat lunch all at the same time. That's how I felt most productive; it kept me revved-up. I competed with myself to see how much

I could accomplish in the shortest amount of time. This adrenaline rush of pushing myself to get more and more done was pretty intense, but because there were so many things I wanted to pack in before I considered it enough, the days kept getting longer and longer. Over time this naturally resulted in personal burnout and, later, a book describing my way back from that chaos toward a saner lifestyle (*How to DeStress Your Life*—still one of the most personal books I've ever written).

It's been a struggle to balance what I learned through that time in my life with the current tantalizing allure of technology. I still hear the siren song that, through this feature or this device, I really can have it all or do it all. And I fight that temptation because the pull is very strong. Most multitaskers I've met are similar.

Somewhere in our cultural history we bought into the fallacy that we could *have* it all. We bought into the related fallacy that we could *do* it all; we actually bought into the notion that we're able to do multiple things at once. As much as I might wish otherwise, it doesn't work like that.

Let's go back to the woman and the fountain. Her brain was engaged in multiple things—walking and texting. Now, obviously, she was able to do at least two things at once, as her walk up to the fountain attests. However, her concentration, her focus, was on only one thing—texting, which requires concentration no matter how fast or how good you are at it. The other thing she was doing, walking, was being done on autopilot. Her brain didn't have to consciously think to put one foot in front of the other. So, had it been a straight, unencumbered walkway, there would have been no viral video. Autopilot would have sufficed, at least until she stumbled into the exit. The difficulty arose when she had to mentally focus on two things simultaneously—texting and *watching where she was going*. Both of these require visual processing. She could not both look at her phone while texting and look up from her phone and see the fountain. The phone won (or, actually, the fountain did); she lost and paid the price for trying to multitask.

We're spending a good portion of our day and many of our activities on autopilot. The question becomes: What price are we paying?

You know you've experienced this. Because you're concentrating so hard on one activity, you put the other task on autopilot. Have you ever been so consumed with what happened at work that you find yourself in your driveway with no real recollection of how you got there? If so, you've driven home on autopilot. You've seen it in others. Have you ever tried talking to your husband while he's reading the paper, only to realize after the third consecutive "uh-huh" that he's tuned out? Your conversation (or at least his side of it) was on autopilot.

We're not actually multitasking. Instead we're spending a good portion of our day and many of our activities on autopilot. The question becomes: What price are we paying for a life on autopilot?

Going online is compelling. There is so much to see and do, so many ways to connect. Maintaining your online presence while simultaneously navigating life requires something called *continuous partial attention,* according to Linda Stone, a former Apple and Microsoft executive, who first coined the phrase. She defines continuous partial attention this way: "to pay continuous partial attention is to pay partial attention—*continuously.* It is motivated by a desire not to miss anything and to be a live node on the network—in touch and seen by others."[2]

It's like having one foot in cyberspace and one foot in "meatspace" all the time. It's not that easy to do, and occasionally you stumble trying to accomplish both. Stone goes on to say, "Continuous partial attention is an always-on, anywhere, anytime, any place behavior that involves an artificial sense of constant crisis. We are always in high alert when we're in constant partial attention." Stone calls attention "the most powerful tool of the human spirit." She says you can enhance it through things like exercise and meditation,

Notable Unsafe Texts

- **On August 29, 2007**, fourteen-year-old Danny Oates was killed by a young driver of a car who was accused of texting while driving. The driver was sentenced to six years imprisonment for vehicular manslaughter.[3]

- **On January 3, 2008**, twenty-six-year-old Heather Leigh Hurd and her fiancé were driving to meet a wedding planner when a tractor-trailer crashed into ten vehicles at a stoplight. The driver of the tractor-trailer was reaching to send a text message. Two people were killed in the accident, including Heather Hurd, and her fiancé was seriously injured. Hurd's father, Russell, has since campaigned for laws banning texting while driving.[4]

- **On September 12, 2008**, a Los Angeles commuter train carrying 220 people collided head-on with a freight locomotive, leaving 25 dead and 138 injured. The commuter train operator had been texting friends as it headed into danger.[5]

- **On May 8, 2009**, a Boston Green Line trolley rear-ended another trolley waiting at a traffic signal, resulting in forty-six injuries and $9.6 million in damages. The driver, twenty-four-year-old Aiden Quinn, was texting his girlfriend when he finally noticed the red lights, but it was too late.[6]

or you can "diffuse it through technologies such as e-mail and Blackberries."

Whether you call it autopilot or continuous partial attention, I'm not sure living this way is all it's cracked up to be. Life is not best lived in "an artificial sense of constant crisis."

When reading over Stone's definition of continuous partial attention, I imagined a pinball machine and a little metallic ball getting thwacked by every new piece of data, careening from subject to subject, unable to stop moving at any one place for any appreciable amount of time. That visual reminded me of the constant energy and motion often exemplified by attention deficit disorder (ADD) or attention deficit hyperactivity disorder (ADHD). If a person is in a constant state of *partial attention*, aren't they are also in a constant state of *partial distraction*?

This media-driven continuous partial attention syndrome may create distractibility as compelling as ADD.

The symptoms of ADD are an inability to maintain focus, to exhibit wandering attention with poor listening skills, and a tendency to overlook details. ADHD adds the component of hyperactivity, fidgeting, and an inability to remain still and calm. The causes of ADD and ADHD are thought to be primarily biological. But what if our tech-obsessed, hypermedia culture injects a component of nurture into this discussion of biology and nature? When ADD and ADHD are biological (nature), their physical imperative for distractibility is difficult to overcome. But this media-driven (nurtured) continuous partial attention syndrome may create distractibility as compelling as ADD. On the one hand, your brain is switching from task to task to task like a Ping-Pong ball because of a *neurological* imperative. On the other hand, your brain is switching from task to task to task like a Ping-Pong ball because of a *learned* imperative. Dr. John Ratey, from Harvard Medical School and author of *Delivered From Distractions*, calls the latter pseudo-ADD[7] or *acquired* ADD.[8]

We may be teaching ourselves to remain in a continually distracted state, with our brains quickly learning the lesson.

BAIT AND SWITCH

Through a recent technology called fMRI (functional Magnetic Resonance Imaging) it's now possible to see what's happening within the brain in real time. We have learned that our brains *are* able to do two things at once, but only if the functions required occur in separate parts of the brain. For example, you can read a book and hear music just fine. One part of your brain handles the visual stimuli from the book while another part of your brain processes the auditory stimuli from the music. There's no interference. But throw in music with lyrics while you're reading, and you have a problem because now the language processing part of the brain is doing double-duty. While the brain can do double duty, it cannot process both things *simultaneously*. Rather, it switches back and forth very, very fast: words on the page to words in the music, words on the page to words in the music. Back and forth, back and forth, switch-switch-switch-switch-switch. Relaxing, right?

The more things we cram into our lives, the more ways we feel obligated to produce.

We can train our brains to switch faster, but the number and complexity of things we're asking our brains to switch back and forth and to and from is increasing. We keep piling on the tasks we're asking our brains to keep track of so we can have it all and do it all. We listen to the promises of how wonderful this is or how time-saving that is and add layer upon layer upon layer to our lives. When the promises are broken, we end up buried under all that stuff, resentful, over-stimulated, and tired. The more things we cram into our lives, the more ways we feel obligated to produce.

The very things we thought were supposed to make our lives easier have turned it into a nightmare. We're getting stressed out.

NOT ME

The obvious answer to all this frenetic activity and stress is to stop doing so much. You'd think we'd understand that we genuinely can't do it all and start limiting our technologies and distractions in order to produce better results. While it would seem obvious, it's actually not—at least not to the people it should be obvious to.

A team of researchers at Stanford University conducted a fascinating study a few years ago looking at two types of people: those self-identified as being heavy media multitaskers (HMM) and those who identified as being low media multitaskers (LMM).[9] The high-octane HMM people assumed they were mentally superior, perhaps because they multitasked all the time. However on cognitive tests, the LMM people, those able to limit or filter out multiple media streams, actually performed better than the HMM subjects. All that heavy media consumption did not produce a positive effect on productivity and output; instead, the effect was negative. Overstimulation produces a cacophony of distractions, and those who use media the most appear to be the most distracted and the least able to filter it out of their lives. Those who were able to "unplug" from competing technological distractions did better on the cognitive tests. Less was actually more.

Apparently, this came as a shock to the HMM group, who considered themselves quite skilled at multitasking. The article I read about the study proposed that this was an example of the Dunning-Kruger effect. The Dunning-Kruger effect, in part, is a condition of *cognitive bias* that occurs when people believe incorrectly in their own superior skill or knowledge and fail to recognize their mistakes. (The bias also describes the reverse, when people incorrectly underrate their abilities.) We are often the worst judge of our own capabilities or lack thereof.

Those who were able to "unplug" from competing technological distractions did better on the cognitive tests. Less was actually more.

I bring this up because I understand the trap of believing that it's not me who is hindering my functioning: maybe I just don't have the right device, or I just haven't found that one gadget, that one app or add-on that will transport me to productivity Nirvana. I don't want to believe that engaging in five things at once and well is a myth. I've come to rely on juggling all those balls in order to get through my day, and I can't even contemplate what life will be like if I don't have access to these tools I need in order to function.

These thoughts are seductive; that anxiety is compelling. We believe that the one thing that's actually hindering us is what will save us. Multitasking is not the answer; it is not the panacea we've been promised. It doesn't lead to greater productivity; it leads to less.

THE TYRANNY OF TMI

This problem with multitasking is not only with multiple media streams, but it's also with the absolute gusher of information flowing from any one of those streams. We're flooded with factoids. The hard drives in our heads are maxed out and need defragmenting.

A national discussion has been going on recently regarding the effects of this technology-driven information onslaught. A recent article in *Newsweek* magazine was entitled "I Can't Think! The Twitterization of our culture has revolutionized our lives, but with an unintended consequence—our overloaded brains freeze when we have to make decisions."[10] The cover for March 7, 2011, read "Brain Freeze: How the deluge of information paralyzes our ability to make good decisions" and showed a man whose head was encased in a large block of ice against a backdrop of line upon line of fine-print text.[11]

The article "I Can't Think!" described what I've witnessed over many years of counseling: the paralysis resulting from overload. People can become overloaded by any number of things: intense emotions, conflicting outcomes, expectations of others, or the pain of the past. But it's a modern phenomenon for people to become overloaded with sheer volumes of information. Whatever the reason, when people get overloaded, they tend to detach. Their situational stress becomes so unlivable they unhook through violent rage, depressive apathy, or a whole range of disorders and destructive behaviors meant to act as release valves to the mounting pressure of their internal conflict.

Overloaded people tend to act in a couple of different ways, both leading to an inability to make rational decisions. The first is to exit the situation; the second is to overreact to the situation. Neither allows for a rational response. Too much marital disharmony? Get a divorce. Too many problems with the kids? Write them off. Too much conflict with a coworker? Quit. Too much work to overcome an addiction? Relapse. Too much trouble to work out a problem? Get angry. Too embarrassed to say you're sorry? Stonewall.

This happens with information overload as well. Each piece of information you take in requires one or more decisions: What will you do with it? Is it useful? Is it trustworthy? How does it fit with the other bits of information you have? Is it the last piece of information you need? In this technological age of flood-stage information, there is a sense that more is best: bring it on. Anything I can learn, I should learn, right? And learning has never been easier than it is today with virtual encyclopedias of knowledge and endless archives of anecdotal tidbits as close as your purse, pocket, or backpack.

There is a principle expressed in Proverbs 11:14 which says, "Where there is no guidance the people fall, but in abundance of counselors there is victory" (NAS). But we've gone so far past abundance that we're now into overload. With so many competing voices, it's impossible to make sense of anything.

Social psychologist Sheena Iyengar, author of *The Art of Choosing*, has conducted research demonstrating that an overload of choices leads to paralysis. In one of her studies she set up a table of jam samples at a California supermarket. On one day there were twenty-four samples to choose from. On another day she laid out six. As a thank-you, samplers on both days were given discount coupons to buy any jam in the store. With twenty-four samples to choose from, you'd think just about anyone sampling would have been able to find something they liked and discounted jam would have flown off the shelves. But the opposite happened: only one out of thirty-three discount coupons were redeemed when there were twenty-four samples. When only six samples were displayed, one out of three samplers purchased a discounted jam.[12] Filtering choices conquers indecision, but overload creates paralysis.

The paralysis of choice in this study was over mere jam, but it applies to just about anything. It takes time and effort to process information and choices. When choice piles up, people mess up. They make impulsive judgments just to get it done, or they hold off deciding, waiting endlessly for that one critical piece of information they desperately hope will bring order to the chaos.

Filtering choices conquers indecision, but overload creates paralysis.

All of that information, all of those tasks, go into a holding pattern like planes at an overbusy airport. The overload produces such a mass of incoming stimuli there's no time for processing or evaluation. Perspective can't bubble up to the surface when insight is weighted down by a glut of information. It's like trying to find your car keys in a messy room you don't even recognize. That one piece of information you need is impossible to find under all those other things. Wading through less is more—especially when what you actually need to tap into isn't more information from the outside but more of who you are from the inside. Decisions aren't always based on bits of data. Instead, they can be made on wisdom, experience, insight, and gut feelings. Wisdom is not just the accumulation of data; it is data's synthesis, and synthesis takes time. (Think of a pyramid with data at the base proceeding upward with information and knowledge, culminating in wisdom at the top. This is also known as the DIKW hierarchy [data, information, knowledge, wisdom]. Wisdom requires having knowledge based on information composed of data, but data alone will not get you there.)

Our information-saturated HMM world promises better decisions and greater insights, but the opposite appears to be true. As much as we'd like to believe otherwise, we weren't designed to do multiple things at once, and we aren't at our best when barraged by data. What all this frenzy and multitasking appears to be best at creating is stress, tension, and a deterioration in our ability to make good decisions.

Wisdom is not just the accumulation of data; it is data's synthesis; and synthesis takes time.

That *Newsweek* article also described two different types of people, *sufficers* and *maximizers*. Sufficers were those able to say "enough": they were the LMM people, the ones who could quell the cacophony. Maximizers, though, were those who couldn't stop taking in information and thus had trouble moving past one decision and onto the next. Paradoxically, the thing we think will lead us one way sends us in the opposite direction. And cognitive bias blinds us to the truth.

Today's maximizing multitaskers sound a great deal like what used to be called type A people. Type A people were high-octane producers, with a "take no prisoners" personality. They were also stressed-out workaholics with quick tempers. They were driven to achieve their stratospheric goals, accompanied by subterranean levels of patience. They made quick, forceful decisions and operated best with a high degree of control over themselves and others. These people were great at business, amassing wealth, and dying young.

Today's tech industry is tailor-made for type A traits. You might even say they're codependent. Type A people love technology because it promises more speed and more control. Technology producers love type A people because, for them, nothing is ever good enough; there's always a desire for more, better, newer, faster...plus a willingness and ability to pay for it. While type A multitaskers are prone to *cognitive bias*, blind to the downside of all this stuff they keep buying more, technology producers suffer from *corporate bias*, blind to the downside of all this stuff they can keep *selling* more. Technology producers will continue to promise and multitaskers will continue to believe. So, how do you exit the rat race?

TUNING OUT

Since we know we can't do multiple things at once—no matter how much we wish and think otherwise—it just makes sense to learn lessons from the LMM group and the sufficers. I know this sounds like heresy to some of you. I can hear your mental objections coming across loud and clear—LMM people are no better than Luddites, rejecting technology out of fear of the unknown. Why would you want to limit anything? Limit is deprivation; it is, well, limiting. The word *suffice* sounds so marginal, so restrictive. Suffice is to technology what diet is to eating. How can I be and do all I need to while hindered by limits and restrictions? I need these things; I need these tools. If you're going to tell me I can't have my cell phone, we're done! You're just a tab away from oblivion on my notebook!

OK, are we done? If this is your reaction, you've just gone zero to sixty in a school zone. Calm down, take a deep breath, and listen.

Have you ever stopped to think how telling it is that the *i* in all these devices is lowercase and the Pad or the Pod is capitalized? It's interesting because they have such a capacity to take over our lives that "I" become lowercase while "it" becomes uppercase in our minds. When we conclude that we absolutely need these things to survive, we cede control to them. We cede peace, security, and surety to them. We become a little "i."

When I think back over the last two decades of my life, I'm amazed at how much things have changed. When did any of these become a genuine need? Are they oxygen or water or food or shelter? I joked earlier about all this technology being the air I breathe, but it's not, not really. If I had to, I could and would find a way to get things done without them. I would find a way to live without a smartphone, an Xbox, a Kindle, or a Bluetooth. I don't truly want to, but neither do I want my life to feel propelled by all this stuff. I want to find a way to coexist sanely with my technologies of choice, where I'm in control instead of being controlled.

When we conclude that we absolutely need these things to survive, we cede control to them.

That's why it's useful to examine the lessons the LMM people and the sufficers can teach us. The low media multitaskers still use media; the difference is they are able to self-limit and self-regulate its use. When it becomes too overwhelming, they know when to staunch the flood. The sufficers still access information, but they stop when they've found what they're looking for. They use internal controls to regulate use and trust themselves to make informed choices rather than trusting sheer information instead.

These people accept the wisdom of focusing on one thing at a time. Rather than being unproductive and time-consuming, they understand this concentrated focus can produce quicker and better results. They understand and accept the way things are instead of

constantly looking for artificial shortcuts. LMM people and sufficers are probably more like the old type B people, the ones who
were said to be more patient, laid back, and less stressed.

It's just so seductive to think you can multitask. But when the
brain has to switch-switch-switch-switch-switch, each realign-
ment from one task to another requires time and mental energy.
The more tired you are, the more stressed you are, and the more
time and energy multitasking takes. Every time you leave task A,
even for a moment, you need to reorient yourself to task B. Switch
back, and this time it's remembering all the aspects of A. Now, try
adding in C and D. Is it possible to do A, B, C, and D? Yes, but
if you mono-tasked, doing A, then B, then C, then D instead of
A-B-A-C-D-B-A-C-D-C-B-D-C-D-B-A, it will probably take less
time overall, be much less stressful, and result in a better product
at the end.

As Abraham Lincoln once famously noted, "Give me six hours
to chop down a tree and I will spend the first four sharpening the
axe."[13] He was probably an LMM-er, of course. Otherwise he might
have chopped, sharpened, chopped, sharpened, chopped, sharpened—and wasted a lot of time with a dull blade and a poorly
chopped tree.

Being There

Multitasking isn't about doing multiple things at once; it's about
managing multiple distractions. Multitasking shatters focus and
concentration. When you're constantly doing A-B-A-C-D-B-A-C-D-
C-B-D-C-D-B-A, you never get to enjoy and focus on A, let alone B
or C or D. They may all get done, but the accomplishment is staccato and the quality is spotty. With your attention diverted to multiple things, you will tend to miss and fail to appreciate all the nuances

of focused activity. Stressed-out, frenetic activity, with the constant switch-switch-switch-switch-switch, becomes the norm. Just like the proverbial frog in the kettle, we boil in the stew of our own stress, oblivious to the rising heat.

In order to help people calm their racing thoughts and learn to focus and appreciate engaging in a single thing, we teach something called mindfulness. Mindfulness has been defined as "the art of being present" and focused in the moment. You intentionally set aside your anticipation, worry, or simple speculation about what might happen in the future; you accept being fully present in the moment. You intentionally set aside any tendency to dwell on the past, regrets, or disturbing memories; you accept being fully present

Family Tasking

After conducting an intensive four-year study of family dynamics, UCLA anthropologist Elinor Ochs noticed that multitasking has dramatically affected modern family dynamics, especially when compared to a similar study conducted twenty years ago. From *Time* magazine's report:

"One of the things Ochs' team of observers looks at is what happens at the end of the workday when parents and kids reunite—and what doesn't happen, as in the case of the Coxes. 'We saw that when the working parent comes through the door, the other spouse and the kids are so absorbed by what they're doing that they don't give the arriving parent the time of day,' says Ochs. The returning parent, generally the father, was greeted only about a third of the time, usually with a perfunctory 'Hi.' 'About half the time the kids ignored him or didn't stop what they were doing, multitasking and monitoring their various electronic gadgets,' she says.

"'We also saw how difficult it was for parents to penetrate the child's universe. We have so many videotapes of parents actually backing away, retreating from kids who are absorbed by whatever they're doing.'"[14]

in the moment. Both past and future concerns can be tyrannical; they crowd out enjoyment in the present.

The technology we've invited into our lives can be tyrannical. Each new device has the tendency to yell, "Hey! Over here! Look at *me!*" They can crowd out enjoyment in the present by hijacking it, by demanding we divert whatever we're doing and pay attention to them. Technology becomes our focus and everything else becomes a distraction handled on autopilot—tasks we dismiss as irrelevant, such as walking, driving, working, talking, or even dealing with other people. Our gadgets and devices are compelling and so user-friendly, we can develop a relationship with them to the exclusion of other people and more important tasks.

Both past and future concerns can be tyrannical, they crowd out enjoyment in the present.

═══ CONNECTION SECTION ═══

It's time for a little self-identification. In this chapter there were a couple of different categories used: *heavy media multitaskers* (HMM) and *low media multitaskers* (LMM); *maximizers* (those who feel a need to take in more and more information in order to make a decision) and *sufficers* (those who stop when they've gained enough information); *type A* (driven, workaholic, quick-tempered, and quick at decisions) and *type B* (laid-back, unconcerned, wait-and-see people). For each of these categories, which one do you tend to be most of the time?

- HMM or LMM?

- Maximizer or sufficer?

- Type A or type B?

When you think about what category you most reflect, I'd like you to consider your stress levels. Life produces stress—it's a given. However, you can contribute to higher or lower levels of stress depending upon your personality. HMM/maximizer/type A people will generally experience higher levels of stress. This isn't to say that LMM/sufficer/type B people don't undergo challenges, struggles, and problems just like everyone else; it's that their reaction to all of this is different.

In a technological age, knowledge is the Holy Grail of power and prestige. In an age of productivity, "getting things done" is kingly. In an instant age, time is money.

Ask yourself some questions:

- How do you feel when you wake up in the morning? Rested or restless?

- Do you have trouble going to sleep at night because you can't seem to turn off your brain?

- What's the first thing you do when you wake up? Do you check your cell phone? Do you sign onto Facebook?

- During the day are you constantly thinking about what you have to do next instead of what you're doing right then?

- Do you feel overwhelmed by the pace of your day and all the things you feel you need to do?

- Do you have difficulty making decisions, or having made a decision, do you have difficulty sticking to it?

- At the end of the day do you feel satisfied with what you've done or just exhausted?

It is so easy to become enamored with all of this technology and truly believe it's making a positive difference in your life. It's what you want to believe, what you've come to need to believe because, if all of this stuff can't truly make your life better, what else is there? In a technological age, knowledge is the Holy Grail of power and prestige. In an age of productivity, "getting things done" is kingly. In an instant age, time is money. This is the essence of the multi-tasking, overtaxed world we live in. It's no wonder the gadgets we create reflect those values.

The question you need to ask yourself is this: Are those honestly the values I want to represent, or is there more to this life?

Chapter 3

THIS IS YOUR BRAIN
ON YOUTUBE

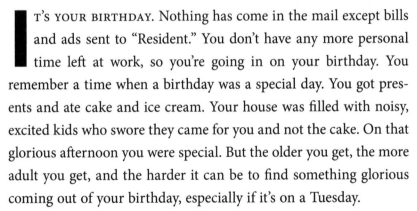

I**T'S YOUR BIRTHDAY.** Nothing has come in the mail except bills and ads sent to "Resident." You don't have any more personal time left at work, so you're going in on your birthday. You remember a time when a birthday was a special day. You got presents and ate cake and ice cream. Your house was filled with noisy, excited kids who swore they came for you and not the cake. On that glorious afternoon you were special. But the older you get, the more adult you get, and the harder it can be to find something glorious coming out of your birthday, especially if it's on a Tuesday.

But wait. You haven't logged on to Facebook yet! The moment you think of it, the dilemma begins. Do you log on to see how many posts you have, or do you just think about how many you have? Once you log on, you'll know; you'll know whether or not anyone stopped long enough to wish you a happy birthday. You hesitate, but once you've asked yourself the question, it's impossible not to answer it. So you log on and cringe, just a bit.

Sweet relief! You have twenty-seven wall posts from people you saw yesterday to people you haven't seen since third grade. There are even friends of friends of friends who have sent along a happy birthday wish. You have not gone unnoticed, even though you still have to show up for work. Someone has noticed, and that feels good.

You have unlimited texting on your phone, so it's no big deal, really. You sign up to receive tweets from the offensive left tackle of your city's NFL team. That's along with all of the other tweets you get—some from people you know but mostly from people you don't. You sign up and then you wait. Before long, there's the tweet! It's not *about* anything significant; that's not the point. The point is you're connected to an elite group of people receiving this special message (albeit numbering in the thousands). But thousands aren't millions, and that somehow makes you feel good.

Facebook popularity feels like hitting the lottery. It feels good, and you want to continue to feel good, so you keep doing it.

It's 6:56 a.m. and you're trying to decide whether or not to say yes to the latest Groupon discount. You're not totally interested in having a facial, but the ad copy is so cleverly written and the description of the business so sassy and fun, you're tempted to join in, out of sheer appreciation for whoever wrote it. And it's a good deal. Sure, it's a little out of your way, but you can't remember the last time you had a facial. OK, maybe you've never had one, so why not now? It seems carefree—catering to your wild side, which, of late, has been noticeably quiescent.

On the other hand, it's a financially good deal, which caters to your practical side. So, with a "what the heck" attitude, you join the group and add your yes to the mix. Even if it doesn't pan out because not enough people join in, it still feels good, maybe as good as the facial.

You know you're not supposed to be surfing the Internet at work, but this thing's only—what—ninety seconds, max? What harm can that be? Well, it did take you longer to find it, but not that long, and you're sure your coworkers haven't seen it yet. After all, they don't spend as much time online as you do and have come to rely on you to handle the techy tidbits. Someone else brings in doughnuts every Thursday, and it's your job to bring in the Net nibble of the week. It all started with those Maru, the Japanese cat, videos. All of you ended up talking about them for weeks. People you hardly spoke to at work came up and asked you to watch them. What's not to like about a fluffy, rotund kitty and all those crazy boxes? Now they look to you for that brief respite of online entertainment. Your coworkers huddle around your computer, look over shoulders, and laugh quietly, watching the latest viral phenomenon. You have value, you have cachet. It feels good.

It does feel good. Each experience like this is like a drug hit, a thrill. Doing this stuff activates your brain's pleasure centers. The more fun it is, the more you want to do it. The more you want to do it, the more you actually do. The more you do, the closer you come to that line, the line over which impulsive activity becomes addictive. It happens with chemicals and substances, and it happens with behaviors such as shopping and gambling. Finding the perfect Internet video feels like locating that must-have item of clothing—on sale. Being successful with a Groupon deal feels like winning the pot in poker. Facebook popularity feels like hitting the lottery. It feels good, and you want to continue to feel good, so you keep doing it.

According to an article in *Time* magazine entitled "Wired for

Distraction: Kids and Social Media," we have two different brain circuits: the first is for concentrating, when we bear down and genuinely focus, and the second is for "reactive attention," when we look up and pay attention to something new or novel.[1] The new and the novel can produce a pleasurable response. Quoting a Stanford researcher, the article says, "Each time we get a message or text, our dopamine reward circuits probably get activated, since the desire for social connection is so wired into us." *Ding!* A message. *Ding!* A text. *Ding!* A factoid or video. Ding, ding, ding. Fun, fun, fun. Twenty years ago someone ringing your doorbell triggered your reactive attention. Ten years ago it was the AOL "You've got mail!" announcement. Now it's a minute-by-minute symphony of chimes, bells, beeps, and growls from every connected device in your life.

HAVING FUN

There is nothing pathological about having fun and about feeling enjoyment. We were created with these feelings and this potential. Engaging in a pleasurable activity is not inherently wrong. But remember the line? The line between activity and addiction lies at the crossroads where an activity that is positive or neutral takes a decidedly negative turn. With addictive behaviors that do not involve chemical substances, there are a series of conditions you can use to determine severity.

Importance: How important has it become to your sense of self and the way you live your life? You can determine importance not only by how much you're doing it but also by how much you're not doing other things. Priority equals importance.

Reward response: Does doing it make you feel better, more in control? Does not doing it make you feel worse? This is that dopamine response referenced earlier. Doing things you enjoy makes you feel better. Avoiding things you dislike can make you feel better, at least initially. There is a positive physical payoff to all this activity that can obscure the negative consequences.

The line between activity and addiction lies at the crossroads where an activity that is positive or neutral takes a decidedly negative turn.

Prevalence: Do you find yourself doing it more often and for longer periods of time than you originally planned? This is the never-enough compulsion that I talked about in another one of my books, *Gotta Have It!* If you feel compelled to say, "Just a little bit more," all the time, you're carving out more and more space in your life for these activities. The question becomes, in order to carve out this time, to what else are you taking the knife?

Cessation: Do you feel anxious or uncomfortable if you cannot do it or if you just think about not doing it? One way to gauge how important these things have become to you is to consider

Digital Epidemic Self-Test

If you know what more than a few of the following phrases refer to, you may be spending too much time online surfing the viral waves![2]

- "Will It Blend?"
- "HeadOn. Apply directly to the forehead."
- *Homestar Runner*
- "I'm a lighthouse. Your call."
- The Neiman Marcus cookie recipe
- "All your base are belong to us."
- Leeroy Jenkins!
- The Dramatic Chipmunk
- "Impossible is nothing."
- Rickroll
- Star Wars Kid

doing without them. Your initial emotional and physical response can be highly instructive. The higher the level of panic and pain you anticipate, the stronger the hold they have over you.

Disruption: Has doing it disrupted your life and your relationships, causing interpersonal or personal conflicts over what you're doing? Imagine your life as a drawer full of those old-school hanging file folders (we use these at work so it's an easy stretch for me). The drawer only has so much space for files. Every time you add a file called "Texting" or "Facebook" or "Checking in" or "Xbox" or "Games," you have to push folders around to find room in the drawer. Inside that drawer are already files called "Sleep," "Family," "Chores," and "Work." Some of the files in your drawer aren't fun; they're thick and heavy and take up a lot of space. The more new stuff you're trying to pack into that drawer of your life, the more pressure it puts on the things and people already there.

Who and what are you shoving aside and jostling to make more room for your tech toys and online interactions?

Reverting: Do you often say to yourself you're going to do something different but then turn around and keep doing the same thing—or doing it even more? This is the "I'll diet again on Monday" syndrome. If you've already made room in your virtual file drawer for something fun and pleasurable or at least distracting, just thinking about depriving yourself of it brings up a wealth of rationales and reasons why "right now" is just not the best time to stop. A part of you may recognize there's an issue, and that part may even gain temporary ascendency; but like a helium balloon it eventually runs out of gas, and those good intentions fall. Before you know it, you're right back to doing what you did, and more.

Impulse Control

Addiction is behavior that controls you. Absent an outside chemical or a substance involved, it's actually *you*—your impulses, your pleasures, your anxieties, your fears, your preferences—taking center stage over your better judgment or reasoned decisions.

The more new stuff you're trying to pack into that drawer of your life, the more pressure it puts on the things and people already there.

It seems to me that the trigger for so much of this technology activity is related to impulse control. An impulse is a thought that prompts action. Impulsivity is where you act on thoughts in the short term whether or not you will benefit in the long term. In the psychology world there is something called *impulse control disorder*, and it comes into play with compulsive behaviors such as stealing, pathological gambling, hair pulling, skin picking, and nail biting. In each the thought behind the impulse is to provide some sort of momentary gain, a hit if you will. The theft of an item or gambling brings relief from the mounting pressure to return to the behavior. Pulling your hair, picking at your skin, or biting your nails is a physical distraction to a psychological distress.

In each of these there is an imperative to the impulse. Do you remember in the last chapter where I said I still feel a compulsion to answer my phone, no matter how peaceful or noninvasive the ringtone is? There is an inner urgency that has nothing to do with the actual content of the call. The impulse is within *me*, not within the call itself. Many of us keep answering the siren call of technology with increasing urgency. We have imbued our devices with elevated importance and have contributed to the constant state of crisis about what we might be missing if we're not online or connected. Our impulse is to always say yes to our technology in order to experience a short-term benefit even if such use results in a long-term loss. But every yes we give technology moves us closer and closer to that line between activity and addiction.

Long View

Most of us are decidedly shortsighted. Our long-term goals generally revolve around what we're going to have for dinner. In a frenetically paced, technology propelled world our time is segmented into fifteen-minute increments. At least that's what a friend of mine always says. She knows what she's doing at the moment and in the next fifteen minutes, but beyond that she can't even calculate because she's overloaded by all the immediate pressures in her life. It's not uncommon for her to miss meetings or forget important dates because she's so engrossed in the *now* that she has no time or energy to give thought to the *then*. She'll get to then when it's about fifteen minutes away. She gets a lot done, but she lives a stressful life. I keep advising her to slow down and take some time to relax. She says she'll relax when she gets everything done, which she never seems to do, and so it goes.

We were created to be chronological creatures, with a past, a present, and a future. Impulsivity tends to anchor us into just one piece of that temporal triad: the present. Note that this is different from the present-focus of mindfulness that I talked about in the last chapter. Being in the moment is quite different than being a hostage of momentary demands. Impulsivity demands relief in the short term, regardless of the consequences. There is a present out-of-control panic to impulsivity while mindfulness intentionally controls the present in order to feed the soul. Mindfulness is about creating a sense of peace, calm, and quiet in the midst of a battlefield of distractions. Mindfulness values the present for what it brings and focuses on fully living in the moment, while impulsivity's only concern with the present is to move past it and on to the next thing.

In order to control our impulses, it's important to integrate the temporal triad of past, present, and future into our decisions. Impulsivity screams "Now! Now! Now!" but we should learn to respond to that imperative by saying, "Not so fast."

Imagine you're driving home and your cell phone goes off. Your immediate reaction is to answer it, but you suddenly realize you left your Bluetooth on your desk at work. What do you do?

- *Option 1:* Take the call and continue driving.

- *Option 2:* Pull over to the side of the road and then take the call.

- *Option 3:* Keep driving, let it go to voice mail, and pick up the message later.

What do you want to do? If you're honest, you're probably going to pick Option 1, take the call and continue driving. What I *want* to do is to drive and talk at the same time. That is my natural inclination, and my impulse is to pick up the phone. "What do you want to do?" is impulsivity's short-term question.

But what *should* you do? That's a longer term question. It's an integrated question, factoring in a variety of components. Depending on where you live, with Option 1 there is always the potential of being ticketed by a police officer for use of a cell phone without a hands-free device. There's also the potential that you'll get so distracted by the call you'll have an accident. There is *risk* involved with Option 1.

With Option 2 you get to answer the call, but you're no longer making forward progress by driving. Option 2 will cost you *time*. Are you late? Do you have a few minutes to spare? Can you explain your situation and let the person know you'll call back when you're at your destination?

With Option 3 you've put off knowing the what and why of the call. Option 3 costs you *immediate knowledge* and necessitates a follow-up. You can't just take care of whatever it is now. Whatever it is will have to wait until you either can't stand it anymore and revert to Option 1 by accessing the message on your cell phone or Option 2 by pulling over so you can figure out if it's something urgent or not.

Wait...It Gets Better

When technology and useful gadgets are constantly on hand to satisfy our every need, interest, and whim, we may not be doing ourselves any favors. We could well be forgetting how to be patient, how to wait, and how to defer gratification. And how to succeed.

"To test the theory of a person's ability to delay gratification, the Stanford Marshmallow Experiment (1972), conducted by Prof. Walter Mischel, at Stanford University, California, studied a group of four-year-old children, each of whom was given one marshmallow, but promised two on condition that he or she wait twenty minutes before eating the first marshmallow. Some children were able to wait the twenty minutes, and some were unable to wait.

"Furthermore, the university researchers then studied the developmental progress of each participant child into adolescence and reported that children able to delay gratification (wait) were psychologically better adjusted, more dependable persons, and, as high school students, scored significantly greater grades in the collegiate Scholastic Aptitude Test."[3]

All of this is too overwhelming to fully evaluate within just a couple rings, so most people, unless they've decided beforehand not to answer a cell phone while driving, will just go with Option 1. But there's your answer, isn't it? Impulses lose their power when you intentionally decide the action you're going to take beforehand and give yourself permission not to give in to the urgency of the impulse.

Intentionality recognizes "What do you want to do?" while factoring in "What should you do?" to arrive at "What you will do." If I am driving without a hands-free device available, I will either pull over safely or continue to drive and pick up the message later. I have considered the risks and have decided, long term, this course of action is best for me. When I have the impulse to pick up the phone, I'll remind myself of my decision. I'll reassure myself that disaster is not going to strike if I either pull over and take a minute to answer the phone or wait a few minutes until I can access my voice mail. I'll remind myself I am still a good person if I don't immediately answer my phone. The expectation that I must answer the phone, again, comes *from within me*, not the phone.

Impulses lose their power when you intentionally decide the action you're going to take beforehand and give yourself permission not to give in to the urgency of the impulse.

I can hear you objecting and bringing up scenarios in which it is truly imperative for you to pick up the phone: "What about if my wife is calling and there's been some sort of accident, or work is calling and there's an emergency?" These are the sorts of messages you hear when you tell your impulses to quiet down. Impulses tend to default to worst-case scenarios to win the day.

If it actually was my wife calling and I didn't answer, she'd hang up and ring again until I picked up. If this happened, I'd know it was something important and out of the ordinary, so I'd immediately pull over and answer the phone.

If there was some sort of emergency at work and I didn't know about it immediately, I have competent people on-site who could make a decision until I accessed the message.

The tyranny of being connected all the time is that you think you have to be in order to function. Being connected starts out feeling good, but you can find yourself arriving at a place where being disconnected now feels bad.

I have to take the long view, even if that means living with self-imposed limits and restrictions and saying no to my impulses.

This brings us in a round-about circle to the start of this chapter where we dealt with how fun all this technology is and how good it makes you feel, how special and connected. Addictions usually start that way; on some level they are pleasurable. But out-of-control behaviors eventually stop being pleasurable; instead of doing them to feel good, you do them in order to avoid feeling bad. Just the act of not doing them starts to feel bad. That fun, pleasurable behavior creates a dependency. In the beginning, life is *more* with it. At the end, life is less without it. The difference is subtle, but it makes all the difference.

I want to continue to experience joy and pleasure engaging in my technology choices. I don't want to end up feeling pressured, worried, and compulsive about them. I want to live in a world where I answer my cell phone because I want to, not because I have to. Simply put: I don't want to ruin this. I don't want to reactivate my crazy, frantic type A personality traits and hard-wire them into my smartphone.

I have to take the long view, even if that means living with self-imposed limits and restrictions and saying no to my impulses.

Over the next several chapters that's what we're going to do—start taking the long view as we look at various online technologies. We'll begin to put them into context, integrating past, present, and future to determine where they fit best in our lives. These things are so much fun; if they stay within the right boundaries, they'll continue to be.

═══ CONNECTION SECTION ═══

I'd like you to think about where you are on the continuum for the various technologies you use:

Positive   **Negative**

10   9   8   7   6   5   4   3   2   1   0

I'd like you to consider every technology or activity you listed in the Connection Section for chapter 1 when you listed all the things you use and do. Rate each of them and explain why you feel that way about each right now.

Go ahead and duplicate the continuum above for each activity. Under the positive side list anything you feel is a benefit: time-savings, connecting to friends, being better able to relate to your kids. Under the negative side list those things that annoy you, bug you, or worry you: having too many things to keep track of, time away from your family, never being able to use it right.

After you've done that, I'd like you to go back and think about that same continuum, only as a snapshot of the day you purchased your gadget or began your activity. Has it moved to one side or the other? Which ones have become more positive in your life? Which ones have become less positive?

Have you discontinued any of these? Did you turn in your smartphone for a regular cell phone? Did you sign up for Facebook and then realize it was more of a hassle to keep track of it? Granted, I'm not anticipating many of you fall into that category, but if that's the case, it means you have the ability to evaluate and self-limit your technology use.

On other hand, if you keep purchasing or adding more and more technology because what starts out positive keeps shifting toward the negative but you're loath to give anything up, that will be instructive too.

If you're the person who is still fully convinced all of these things are totally positive, I'd like you to reevaluate, using the components I used earlier:

- *Importance:* How important has it become to your sense of self and the way you live your life?

- *Reward response:* Does doing it make you feel better, more in control, and does not doing it make you feel worse?

- *Prevalence:* Do you find yourself doing it more often and for longer periods of time than you originally planned?

- *Cessation:* Do you feel anxious or uncomfortable if you cannot do it or if you just think about not doing it?

- *Disruption:* Has doing it disrupted your life and your relationships, causing interpersonal or personal conflicts over what you're doing?

- *Reverting:* Do you often say to yourself you're going to do something different but then turn around and keep doing the same thing or doing it even more?

Just because something feels good, fun, and pleasurable in the short term doesn't mean it's going to pan out that way in the long run. Staying alert will help you stay in control.

Chapter 4

THANK YOU FOR BEING A FRIEND

THE ARCHAIC DEFINITION of *friend,* according to *Merriam-Webster,* is "one attached to another by affection or esteem."[1] That was before the advent of online social networking. Previously, *friend* was a noun. Friend was what you *were* not what you *did.*

When friend was a noun, it described someone you knew well and liked, and vice versa. Friends spent time together, if not physically then in communication with each other. They shared their lives, their thoughts, their time. *Friend* was distinct from *associate* or *acquaintance.* A friend was a buddy not a colleague. Being a friend had a special connotation of affection and intimate closeness.

A friend was someone who would tell you not to buy that shirt because it absolutely didn't work for you at all.

A friend was someone who would stay with you through the bottom half of the last inning when your team was losing—badly.

A friend was someone who would go out with you for ice cream when you truly needed it and talk you out of it when you didn't.

When friend was a noun, it described someone you knew well and liked, and vice versa.

A friend was someone who wanted to be with you as much as you wanted to be with him.

A friend was someone who knew your secrets and kept them.

A friend was someone who knew your fears and understood them.

A friend was someone hurt by your weaknesses but remained your friend.

There was substance when friend was a noun. Friendship, as a concept, has been proclaimed, acclaimed, and waxed about lyrically in poem and prose for thousands of years. Friend as a noun has existed for a long time.

Here are a few things others have said about friends through history:

> What is a friend? A single soul dwelling in two bodies.[2]
>
> —ARISTOTLE

> A real friend is one who walks in when the rest of the world walks out.[3]
>
> —WALTER WINCHELL

> A true friend stabs you in the front.[4]
>
> —OSCAR WILDE

> It's the friends you can call up at 4:00 a.m. that matter.[5]
>
> —MARLENE DIETRICH

A true friend never gets in your way unless you happen to be going down.[6]

—ARNOLD GLASOW

I value the friend who for me finds time on his calendar, but I cherish the friend who for me does not consult his calendar.[7]

—ROBERT BRAULT

Lots of people want to ride with you in the limo, but what you want is someone who will take the bus with you when the limo breaks down.[8]

—OPRAH WINFREY

Wounds from a friend can be trusted, but an enemy multiplies kisses.[9]

—KING SOLOMON

FRIEND AS VERB

Using *friend* as a verb is a recent phenomenon, thanks to Facebook. According to its website, Facebook users average about 130 friends each.[10] Some people attempt to accumulate friends like other people collect movie ticket stubs: for no real reason except it seems fun to have so many. I'm not sure how you can genuinely keep track of all those people. Having friends on Facebook begets more friends as friends of friends send further friend requests. Like cellular mitosis, that little circle of a few Facebook friends can morph into a much larger mass and become, ultimately, less manageable and decidedly less intimate. How many people can you realistically be friends with? Perhaps there was a reason Jesus had twelve disciples, and spending time with them *was* His day job.

In a verb world *friending* is a simple click, but in a noun world *being a friend* has some time-intensive substance.

In 1993 Robin Dunbar, an anthropologist at the University College of London, conducted research to determine the cognitive limit of a person's effective real-world social network, where individuals know who each person in that network is and how each relates to every other person. His research was based primarily on animal and primate interactions. But Dunbar's analysis and theories have since been applied in psychological and sociological circles and have given rise to "Dunbar's number."[11] That limit, it seems, is about 150 people—including your favorite barista, the gas station attendant, your boss, your employees, people you attend church and social functions with, classmates, and so on. But that's just the limit of people you can maintain *stable relationships* with, much less friendship.

But can you grow your *monkeysphere* (a humorous term applied to this real-world social network) aggressively without harming your closest relationships? If Professor Dunbar is right, our brains just aren't big enough to hold all the information necessary to maintain relationships with multiple hundreds or even thousands of people: the larger your "network," the shallower your connections have to be with each member in your circle.

It takes time to cultivate friendship. In a verb world *friending* is a simple click, but in a noun world *being a friend* has some time-intensive substance.

- *Trust:* Of all the attributes of a true friendship, I
  think this one is foundational. Friends trust each

other because each has proven to be trustworthy.
When tempted to betray the friendship in some way,
they have held fast to the needs and feelings of the
other instead.

- *Honesty:* One of the hallmarks of true friendship is
living within an atmosphere of truth. This truth, however, is not a harsh, brutal presentation but one done
in love, compassion, and tenderness. To a friend the
truth is not a weapon; it is a balm. There is safety in
the honest words of a friend, even when those words
hurt, as Solomon earlier attests from Proverbs 27:6.

- *Understanding:* True friends understand each other.
They know the background and context of each other's lives. They know the *what* of things, but they also
know the *why* of things. Friends know which way the
other will jump and how far.

- *Acceptance:* Friends understand the precarious
position they put themselves in by being a friend.
Proximity sometimes equates to pain where human
beings are concerned; friends acknowledge this as an
acceptable consequence of the friendship.

- *Mutual benefit:* True friends add to each other's lives.
Often the benefit isn't always equal, but it is mutual.
True friends monitor the relationship to ensure there
is both give and take, refusing to allow it to become
chronically one-sided and draining.

- *Sacrifice:* Having said what I did above, there are
times when friendship calls for sacrifice. It can be

sacrifice of time, money, energy, resources—a reordering of priorities to put the needs of the friendship first.

- *Affection:* At the heart of all friendships should be genuine affection one for the other. Friends enjoy each other; they like to be together because of the way they feel about each other.

Like crops on Farmville, friendships wither without cultivation.

Being a friend takes effort. Over time it may seem effortless because of how well you know each other, but any good friendship requires work. It's the same with any close relationship. It may be fun to have 130 friends on Facebook, but how many of those would take you to the airport to catch a 6:00 a.m. flight on a Wednesday? How many of those would actually pick up the phone to call after you'd lost your job? How many would you trust to watch your kids—or feed your fish, for that matter?

Being a friend takes time. Noun friends want to spend time together. They like each other. They make each other a priority. They will put off doing other things, being with other people, in order to spend time together. Like crops on Farmville, friendships wither without cultivation.

REDEFINITION

Charles Cooper, an executive editor at CBS News, received an e-mail from an old work acquaintance one morning, explaining a dire situation she found herself in: she needed money. He would have immediately tagged the e-mail as a hoax except he had just reconnected and friended her on Facebook a few days before. So he logged in, saw she was on Facebook too, and began a real-time chat conversation with her. She reiterated her plea for money, giving credence to the e-mail. However, he became skeptical when the woman's personality didn't match what he remembered of her from the past. After a few carefully worded questions, he knew the Facebooker was not who she claimed to be. He, of course, refused to send her any money and ended the conversation.

Before long Cooper tracked down the real woman and explained the situation. He wasn't the only one who had been targeted for this look-alike scam, including family of the woman who ended up chatting with the imposter online just as he had. In her message to him the real woman said, "I think it's a great cautionary tale...I can see how easy it could be for someone to say just enough to make folks think it really was me. Very scary, this Internet thingie!"[12]

Just because social networks have redefined the word *friend*, you don't have to. It can be dangerous to give that many people that much access into your personal life. It can be dangerous to assume a depth of relationship that doesn't exist. The person you're friending may not actually be who you think they are at all.

But that's the problem, isn't it? You've put yourself out there on Facebook, Twitter, Google Plus, YouTube, or another social networking site. You've spent time and energy creating your profiles, and you want people who know you to have access. You don't honestly think that the friend of a friend of a friend could be so bad, and besides, it's fun to keep track of your friend count: it's a measurement of personal significance. It's fun to have friends and to be a friend. This is just a larger, global community; this virtual circle is just an augmentation of your physical circle of friends. Nobody takes it seriously, right? It's just fun.

Of course, it's not so fun to be defriended or unfriended or exfriended. There's also that awkward situation where you've put out a request to someone to be his or her friend and the request, somehow, never gets answered. Unanswered friend requests mean you are neither in nor out; you are neither hot nor cold; you are the lukewarm milk left untouched. You're perpetually on the hook, waiting for an answer, waiting to know if you've been friended.

Apparently this happens a lot. Millions of unanswered friend requests are swirling endlessly in the back eddies of cyberspace, never reaching fulfillment. Before there were only two options to a friend request: yes or no. But people felt no was way too harsh, too confrontational, too committal, so the wisdom of the crowd came up with that third request-limbo option—don't say no but just never say yes. The situation had to be addressed, of course, so some bright mind at Facebook solved the problem. Now you can click "Not Now" to put a hold on the request indefinitely: institutionalized friend purgatory. Of course, in retribution, you can also withdraw your friend request if it hasn't been accepted—a digital "so there!"

Unanswered friend requests mean you are neither in nor out; you are neither hot nor cold; you are the lukewarm milk left untouched.

This may all take place in the alternate reality known as the Internet, but you're still dealing with real people, expectations, and preferences. It's just that the unwritten social rules are still evolving. It's awkward enough to figure out how to deal with people face-to-face, to decide who to spend time with, how reliable and trustworthy they are, and how many more friends you can squeeze in time for. The ease of just clicking "yes" to more and more friends online isn't actually helping. You're just adding on layers of people who call themselves your "friend," whatever that means to them. It's fluid and changing, constantly being refined and revised, pushed along by the collective experiences of hundreds of millions of people.

And all you wanted to do was find a way to share your Mt. Rushmore pictures with Aunt Helen in Bismarck.

SOCIAL NETIQUETTE

Now you can get in a fight with your friend face-to-face, or you can undergo the drama of unfriending someone or being defriended yourself via social networking. It's hard enough sometimes to keep your temper and your tongue in check with those who are physically present. Now you need to worry about firing off that blistering or embarrassing post, only to realize a coworker or a boss has access to not only the stupid things you say when you're at work but also when you're not. People are losing their jobs or cannot even get hired over what they write and the pictures they post. Now you have to worry about hurting someone's feelings by putting off a friend request from someone who moved away twenty years ago and never bothered to stay in touch.

There is no such thing as anonymity when you're on the grid. You are known and findable.

Then there's that interesting conundrum with parents and teens. Teens love social media because of the freedom it gives them to be themselves and to create an independent identity from their parents. Imagine their chagrin when said parents demand to be friended, or else. What do you do if your teen absolutely refuses to friend you or only gives you limited access? Some kids have reluctantly given their parents access only to defriend them later out of spite over an argument or their absolute embarrassment over the comments being posted by their parents for everyone to see. How can you create an independent identity when your mom posts a comment about your history assignment not being done or starts leaving dorky tags on your real friends' photos?

There is no such thing as anonymity when you're on the grid. You are known and findable.

Facebook not only creates the chimera of relationship, but it also can complicate face-to-face relationships. How do you handle all these situations? Some people have decided the answer is to create an entirely new profile, just not on Facebook. While reading an article about Jimmy Kimmel's call for an "Unfriend Day"—a day where you go through your Facebook friends and cull the herd—I found information about a new social networking site called Path that had just opened up. Within Path's parameters you're only allowed a maximum of fifty friends. The cofounder of Path, Dave Morin, said, "I don't agree that people should unfriend people on Facebook. But I do think it means there is a need for a new kind of service that allows you to share personal moments that are meaningful between you and your closest friends."[13]

What? Wasn't that what Facebook was for? Now I need to go onto another site, set up another profile just for my up-to-fifty friends and family? What happens to my Facebook page? I've already got multiple e-mail accounts; now I need multiple social networking accounts? How many hours do you think I have in my day? If I'm average, Facebook already lays claim to an entire day a month out of my life as it is!

Isn't that the way it always starts, though? At first the new technology seems like the coolest thing in the world—you just have to do it because it's fun and trendy and you don't want to be left out. Then, over time, it's not cool anymore; it's drudgery. You have to do it because you started it and people are expecting it. Sure, it's still fun, but it's taking a lot more time and energy than you ever thought it would. Before you did it because you wanted to, and now you do it because you're sure other people want you to. Maintaining your online presence is like continuing a never-ending chain letter: you imagine

Fee, Fie, Follower... Friend?

"Among the new meanings added to the 12th edition of the *Concise [Oxford Dictionary]* is one for *follower*, 'someone who is tracking a particular person, group, etc. on a social networking site.' In dictionaries of current English some senses which have fallen into disuse have to be removed to make way for new ones such as this: for example, we no longer give the first edition's sense of 'man courting maidservant.' Another new sense is at *friend*, where the primary meaning hasn't changed much since the first edition, though the definition there has a poetic quality that the current one perhaps lacks: 'one joined to another in intimacy & mutual benevolence independent of sexual or family love.' It's the secondary senses that have changed—the new meaning is 'a contact on a social networking website,' while the first edition had 'person who acts for one, e.g. as second in duel.'"[14]

dire consequences if you're the one who stops. You have all these friends now, and you feel you'll disappoint them if you don't keep up. They expect you to post pictures and maintain the dialogue. Before long you're saying things like, "I've got to do my laundry," "I've got to mow my lawn," "I've got to go grocery shopping," "I've got to update Facebook." Life goes from a want-to to a got-to.

Maintaining your online presence is like continuing a never-ending chain letter: you imagine dire consequences if you're the one who stops.

CULLING THE HERD

Noun friends take up enough time and energy just to maintain, strengthen, and grow. Noun friends should take precedence over verb friends. So I think I'm with Jimmy Kimmel on this one. I think it's time to engage in a little herd culling, a little pruning. It's time to recognize that Facebook has a different definition of friend than the traditional one. Consider the ease with which you become a friend, and that will help you determine the depth of that friendship. You start with a great idea, allowing family and friends access to your life—what you're doing, how you're feeling, what's important to you. You desire to be known. That's not a bad thing, but you're not obligated to let just anyone peer through your metaphorical front window. If you truly don't know that person, why would you give him or her that much access into your life?

The reason you don't mind sharing all that personal stuff with family and friends is because you already know them. You have an existing relationship that can be enhanced by the level of sharing that goes on over Facebook. There is already a foundation there, a relationship that's been secured, vetted, and established. Inviting family and friends to the party isn't the problem; it's what happens when practical strangers show up.

Facebook, Twitter, LinkedIn, Flickr, Foursquare, and so on are not intimate, closed, personal circles. The difficulty arises not from your motivations but from the medium. Just mess up setting your security parameters, and hundreds of millions of people have just been invited into your life. You may think being one person in a sea of billions gives you cover—after all, with so many online, who is going to take the time to target you? You'd be surprised. Facebook scams are rising, and people are becoming more and more clever in how they present them.

You may be the type of person who allows only family and friends to gain access. But over time, as more and more people find you and send a friend request, it could become easier and easier to relax those boundaries. After all, it's uncomfortable to outright reject someone who wants to be your *friend*. This can be especially true if they're counting on six degrees or less of separation. So you end up easing out that circle just a little wider with every request. After all, you have one or more friends in common, so you're kind of like a large, extended, virtual family, right? Unfortunately, the third cousin on your mother's father's side, once removed, though technically family, may not be a nice person.

With all of these people comes a sense of obligation. Plus, if you're the type of person who sends thank-you notes for birthday cards, this could be a big problem. Obligating yourself to maintain contact with 130 or more people is a big job. It's going to require a lot of time. That day-a-month thing before long could seem like nothing. It's like spreading yourself a mile wide and an inch deep.

That's not how I define friendship. True friendship is deeper than that. True friendship is a noun.

Inviting family and friends to the party isn't the problem; it's what happens when practical strangers show up.

CONNECTION SECTION

I'd like you to think about who you consider a friend and why. To do that, I'd like to use the noun descriptions of a friend listed earlier in the chapter. For each quote consider whose name you'd use to fill in the blank:

Aristotle said that a friend is a single soul dwelling in two bodies. Who do you consider that close, that intimate, of a friend?

Walter Winchell said a real friend is someone who walks in when the rest of the world walks out. In your life, when you've been rejected by just about everyone else, who stood by your side? Who would stand up for you today?

Oscar Wilde said a true friend stabs you in the front. Who is it that will confront you, even hurt you, to your face?

Marlene Dietrich said it's the friend that you can call at 4:00 a.m. that matters. Who are your 4:00 a.m. friends?

Arnold Glasow said a true friend never gets in your way unless you happen to be going down. Think back over your life. Which friends warned you against harmful actions or tried to stand in your path when you were headed the wrong way?

Robert Brault said he valued the friend who found time on his calendar for him, but he cherished the friend who did not even consult his calendar. Who are your valued friends (those who will find time for you), and who are your cherished friends (those who don't think about the time when it comes to you)? Both are needed and necessary.

Oprah Winfrey reminded us that lots of people want to ride with you in the limo, but what you want is someone who will take the bus with you when the limo breaks down. When's the last time your "limo" broke down? Who took the bus with you?

King Solomon, in Proverbs, said wounds from a friend can be trusted, but an enemy multiplies kisses. We all know those people who will lie to our face because they don't genuinely care about us. Who are the people in your life who can be trusted to tell you even what you don't want to hear?

There are layers to friendship, just like family. My immediate family is my wife and sons. After that are my parents, my sister and brother, and their families. After that are cousins and aunts and uncles, the extended crowd you generally see only at weddings, funerals, and family reunions. For myself, I have a handful of truly close friends whom I keep in contact with regularly. After that are those I enjoy being with but don't see as often. Beyond that is a larger group of people whom I consider friends, but who are more than mere acquaintances but less than intimates. There's an inner circle, a middle circle, and an outer circle. Based on how you've just answered the questions above, whom would you place in each ring?

Now, think about the people you've placed in these circles; where do you think *they* would place *you*? Do you have reciprocity, or are some of your friendships one-sided? As you think of yourself as a friend, go back to the attributes listed in this chapter: trust, honesty, understanding, acceptance, mutual benefit, sacrifice, and affection. How are you doing in each of those categories? Is there one that tends to lag behind the others in how you express friendship? Ralph

Waldo Emerson said that the only way to have a friend is to be one. The depth of your character is best gauged by the depth of your friendships.

Keep your friends as a noun, and resist the lure of friend as merely a verb.

Don't be deceived by this mile-wide-inch-deep verb definition on Facebook; that is not the standard to which you should aspire. Keep your friends as a noun, and resist the lure of friend as merely a verb.

Chapter 5

JUST LIKE REAL LIFE

CHRIS WAS RUNNING late again. It seemed like he was always late. The things he didn't want to do always took longer than he thought, while the things he really wanted to do sucked up time like a huge vacuum hose. There weren't enough hours in the day to do what he had to do and still leave time to do the things he wanted to. It didn't seem fair.

If it were up to Chris, he'd spend all day at home on his computer. He was never bored checking Facebook: there was always something to do, to see, games to play. Work was something he *had* to do, something that took time away from what he *wanted* to do. As usual he was late because he'd gone online for "just a few minutes"; now he was scrambling to get to work on time.

There weren't enough hours in the day to do what he had to do and still leave time to do the things he wanted to.

It wasn't like he even wanted to go to work. Craig hated his job, but it paid for what he needed, not the least of which was Internet access and a cell phone with a data plan. At work he had to do what other people wanted him to do, when they wanted him to do it, how they wanted him to do it. It's not like it was rocket science—how many ways could you break down a cardboard box? All day long he stocked shelves and packed other people's stuff into flimsy grocery bags, suffering through endless hours of smiling and telling people where the pancake syrup was and on which aisle to find the two-for-one snack crackers.

So he developed a game he played at work, a way to pass the time. He tried to make himself as transparent as possible by showing nothing of himself and reflecting only what others wanted. Ask him a question and he provided it, without investing any of his personality into the response. Need directions and he showed the way, listening to the chatter about why they couldn't find something clearly marked in the same place for years with a noncommittal smile. Directed to clean up a spill, he did so without comment, never revealing how much it bugged him that no one else ever got called.

The goal was to reveal nothing of himself, nothing of his personality—not that anyone at work cared anyway. He wasn't there because of who he was; he understood that. He was there because of what he could do. He was a body; he could have been anybody and it would have been fine as far as his coworkers cared, or the shift manager, or the woman in the parking lot who rolled the grocery cart at him so she wouldn't have to walk it back to the store. No one seemed to want to know him or have any sort of interest in who he was, so Chris blandly, intentionally, returned the favor. He was just doing time, waiting for his real life to begin as soon as he got off work and got online.

Virtual Reality

I've always loved books and reading. As a kid I could lose myself for hours in an exotic faraway place, transported by the combination of someone else's written word and my own imagination. There was the real world I lived in and a secondary place I could go if given the time, solitude, and the power of a good book.

Reading has always been a participatory experience, as opposed to television, which is more of a spectator sport. Reading stimulates the imagination; television supplies it for you. Going online is also engaging and participatory. Content is not merely presented to you in twenty-two-minute increments. Instead *you* determine where to go, what to take notice of, and what to disregard. *You* decide if you want to watch that commercial or not; *you* determine if you want to hit that link or view that page. You are in charge of your online content; it's you, in the driver's seat, choosing your own direction.

Gaming can be even more engaging. The graphic and audio sophistication of Internet games is truly mind-boggling. It both activates and tricks the senses. But it's not just how things look and sound; it's also how things feel. So much of what is done on the Internet can simulate reality because of how real it looks. This intensity of experience creates a virtual reality.

There was the real world I lived in and a secondary place I could go if given the time, solitude, and the power of a good book.

The word *virtual* is an interesting one. Once, its primary meaning had to do with something having potential, something possible but not quite actualized. *Merriam-Webster's* first definition of virtual is: "being such in essence or effect though not formally recognized or admitted."[1] To say something was *virtually impossible* meant it was almost impossible but not quite. Virtual meant as close to *actual* as you could get while still retaining the understanding that it was not.

The word *virtual* and the word *reality* were first linked together in the late 1930s when describing the fictitious and illusory reality created on the theatrical stage. But the phrase has left the arts and is now firmly embedded in the techno-lexicon. *Virtual* has become a computer word. Virtual reality (VR) has come to mean a computer-simulated environment of either a real or imaginary place. I remember hearing it the first time while watching people who wore what looked like welder's goggles; they seemed to be randomly moving like puppets on strings, interacting with something only they could see. Now there are entire virtual worlds, worlds that exist only as computer-simulated environments. There are virtual communities, social networks of people connected to each other online. There are even virtual relationships, relationships that exist only online with no physical interaction whatsoever. Virtual reality is almost like the real thing but not quite. The gap between the real and the not-quite, however, keeps getting smaller in the virtual realm, as technology advances. These not-quite experiences are still good enough for many purposes for many people.

ESCAPE HATCH

The Internet can be one enormous escape hatch. When life becomes too hard and stressful, when relationships become too unfulfilling or unsatisfactory, it's compelling to jump down the rabbit hole of the Internet into a world of virtuality. Do you understand it isn't totally real? Yes. But compared to how bad real life feels at the moment, you'll take virtual life anyway, thank you very much. Considering the amount of personal control you have over this almost-real world compared to the lack of control felt in the real one, it's tempting to consider virtual an acceptable trade-off.

Escape hatches can be important things. If your way is blocked out of a dangerous situation, an escape hatch can save your life. Escape hatches, though, are meant to be used sparingly and only at great need. Generally they're not the ideal way to make an exit.

If the Internet has become your personal escape hatch from life as you know it, I'd encourage you to think about why that is. When you use the hatch, what are you escaping from? How effective is it, if you have to keep using it again and again? When you use it, where do you end up? Are you more interested in running away from something than you are in arriving somewhere else?

Compared to how bad real life feels at the moment, you'll take virtual life anyway, thank you very much.

Using an online escape hatch doesn't only mean immersing yourself in games, although that's certainly a compelling avenue to take. Creating an alternative reality isn't just for those with avatars in virtual worlds. Living a virtual life is possible while going about your day job. Living a virtual life happens when you start to put more value in the experiences you create online than the ones encountered in real life. Living a virtual life happens when you step out of the truth of your life and begin to create a false life online.

I learned an interesting fact the other day about Japan and Facebook. Facebook is a global phenomenon. You'd think the techno-friendly Japanese culture would embrace it like so many others. Not so. According to an article in the *New York Times*, of the almost 600 million members on Facebook, fewer than 2 million are from Japan. Less than 2 percent of Japan's Internet population use Facebook compared to more than 60 percent of American's online user base. One reason is that competitors in the Japanese marketplace pre-date Facebook's foray into that country—Miki, Gree, and Mobage-town, each with over 20 million users. But another, more interesting reason is in how the Japanese relate to their social networking sites. In Japan, people apparently do not use their real names online; they use pseudonyms or nicknames. Since Facebook requires members to use real names, it's not very popular. Twitter, on the other hand, does not require authenticity and is growing rapidly.[2]

Living a virtual life happens when you start to put more value in the experiences you create online than the ones encountered in real life.

Japanese users value an online life intentionally divorced from their real life. As one young woman said in the article, "I don't want to give it my real name. What if strangers find out who you are? Or someone from your company?" In her online world she doesn't have to worry about people knowing who she really is. Cloaked in secrecy, she is free to express what she honestly thinks. The article referenced a survey in which nine out of ten Japanese respondents said they were "reluctant to disclose their real names on the Web." Further, the article noted, "Specialists say that while Facebook users in the United States tend to recreate real-life social relationships online, many Japanese use Web anonymity to express themselves, free from the pressures to fit into a conformist workplace."

They don't want to be known for who they are in real life; they value cyber-camouflage.

HIDING IN PLAIN SIGHT

That article got me thinking about how we actually use Facebook and if we're as transparent and open as we think we are.

A woman I know with two small children is going through a difficult time in her life right now: she's getting a divorce. Her husband left her abruptly, leaving her few options but to return to her hometown to live with her parents until she gets "settled." Returning home feels to her like admitting defeat, like she's unable to make it on her own. It's hard for her to think about starting over in life, in relationships, in work; the whole thing is pretty overwhelming.

I started noticing that whenever I'm on Facebook, so is she. I wondered, What are the odds of that? I'm on at pretty random times, but when I am, she's usually on too. You can kind of track her day by when she posts. She's always writing messages and tagging photos. She's put up hundreds of pictures of her kids (they are truly cute) but much fewer of herself. Over the past year she's put on probably thirty pounds, but you'd never know that by her Facebook photos. Her carefully chosen visual representations of herself online are of a much younger, much thinner person.

Looking at her pictures and postings, you'd think nothing was amiss in her life. She writes with superlatives and enthuses about how much fun she's having. Everything is wonderful; everything is good. If I didn't know the reality of her situation, I'd have no way to detect the discontinuity between what's going on in her real life and what she portrays in her virtual life. For portrayal is the right word: she is acting as if everything is fine. Online, her virtual world is positive; off-line, it's awash in stress and decisions, difficulties and disappointments. It's no wonder she spends so much time online.

She has created an avatar, just as much as the users in Japan. Her avatar goes by her real name; it even looks like her, but the image is carefully crafted and controlled. She is hiding in plain sight.

This hiding in plain sight isn't something new; I've seen people do it by saying they're "fine" when they're not. I've seen people carefully create an image through the artful use of hair color, cosmetics, and fashion. I've seen people do it through sports cars, boats, and jet skis. These are props in a staged show allowing the players to maintain the illusion that the façade represents real life. Similarly, the Internet can become another staged production where what is presented is engaging and compelling but ultimately is not the total picture.

All of which brings

> ## Top 15 Most Popular Social Networking Sites
>
> Based on an average of site traffic and estimated unique visitors each month, here are the top 15 social networking sites in late 2011.[3] Which ones do you have a profile on?
>
> - **Facebook**: 700,000,000 visitors
> - **Twitter**: 200,000,000 visitors
> - **LinkedIn**: 100,000,000 visitors
> - **MySpace**: 80,500,000 visitors
> - **Ning**: 60,000,000 visitors
> - **Google Plus**: 32,000,000 visitors
> - **Tagged**: 25,000,000 visitors
> - **Orkut**: 15,500,000 visitors
> - **Hi5**: 11,500,000 visitors
> - **MyYearbook**: 7,450,000 visitors
> - **Meetup**: 7,200,000 visitors
> - **Badoo**: 7,100,000 visitors
> - **Bebo**: 7,000,000 visitors
> - **MyLife**: 5,400,000 visitors
> - **Friendster**: 4,900,000 visitors

me back to the concept of virtual life as opposed to real life. According to author Erik Davis, the term *virtual reality* was first used by French playwright and director Antonin Artaud in 1938. In his book *The Theatre and Its Double*, Artaud used the term *la réalite virtuelle* to describe the effect theatre has on the mind's imagination, "in which characters, objects and images take on the phantasmagoric force of alchemy's visionary internal dramas."[4] It is a world in which what you imagine comes to life. Or, as Shakespeare said in *As You Like It*, "All the world's a stage, and all the men and women merely players."[5]

The Internet has merely provided us with another compelling and engaging stage where we can place ourselves front and center.

The more stressful your life is, the more of a draw virtual diversions become.

FANTASY

In childhood, flights and diversions into a fantasy world have a great deal of meaning and value. That fantasy world of the imagination is all about learning the joy of stretching one's mind beyond what you can see and touch. It's all about learning how to think beyond where you are right now and learning how you might react in a given situation. It is learning simply how to play and create out of nothing more than the contents of your own imagination.

For adults, fantasy can become less about learning how to prepare for reality and more about how to escape from it. Children create fantasy to practice who they will be; adults create fantasy to hide from who they are. This is the potent snare that the Internet and online activities represent. It is not merely the diversion provided through the sheer amount of time online and away from having to deal with your real life. It is also about the content of the illusion you seek to create and maintain online, from the carefully constructed "you" on Facebook to the avatars you incarnate on gaming sites. The more stressful your life is, the more of a draw virtual diversions become.

We all want to better ourselves; it's part of growing up. By understanding and confronting our weaknesses and faults, we work toward growing beyond them and becoming better people. In this case the journey is at least as important as the destination. Invaluable life lessons are learned along the way to personal improvement.

Virtual reality is alluring because it avoids the nuts and bolts of true reality.

The Internet, however, provides a deceptive dead-end disguised as a shortcut. Online, personal improvement can come at the click of a mouse, an improvement of status, the posting of a flattering photo. There is no journey to take, no struggle, no lesson, only the appearance of arrival—smiling and thirty pounds thinner. Online you can claim to be better than you actually are, and most people cannot know the difference. You can claim to be whatever you think you should be, deceiving both yourself and others.

Virtual reality is alluring because it avoids the nuts and bolts of true reality. It sanitizes the situation, bleaching out the problems and frustrations, leaving a spotless canvas upon which to paint an impossible portrait of life. Reality doesn't have that option. It can't duck paying the bills, cleaning the garage, dealing with the boss, coping with an angry spouse, battling the flu, putting on weight, or confronting a disobedient child. In a virtual world you only have to deal with the challenges you want to face, when you want to, how you want to. In a virtual world you can choose to deal only with the challenges that don't matter because they're not really real. It's why virtual reality is more game than life.

You Don't See Me

Ironically, though, in this world of finger-stroke falsehoods and truth avoidance, some people are *more* honest in their written thoughts online than they are in person. It's as if they believe there is some sort of protection given to what a person writes, not what a person says. There is also the erroneous assumption people make regarding their privacy in a virtual world—which is to say, there is none.

I saw a weird story out of England about a teenager who pled innocent to a charge of malicious mischief at his local library. In court he answered "Not guilty" as to whether or not he stopped up all the toilets, flooding the library, causing more than $200,000 damage. Yet when someone asked him about it on Facebook, he admitted he did it. That was all the prosecutor needed. Case closed.[6]

Since the beginning of the Internet there has been this false shroud of anonymity over activities online. People think because they act in semi-darkness, in a basement or closed-door den, no one is going to know what happens. They think that something they write to one person will automatically stay here. This is an illusion. Nothing we do online is anonymous. Someone, somewhere knows. Your spouse may not know, but Google does.

People may forget your latest slip of the tongue, but your slip of the keyboard may haunt you forever.

Every time you access a website, you leave a digital fingerprint. You can erase it from your browser's history, but that's just data on your hard drive (and even that survives simply clearing your cache). Personally identifying information will still reside "out there" on servers all the way from your local ISP to the Web server you accessed to numerous routers in between, scattered all around the globe. Posts removed on Tuesday are still in memory caches from Monday. And if Google, Bing, or the Internet archive managed to snag your post before you deleted it, it will live on forever. Unringing a bell would be easier, in fact, than unsending an ill-sent email. People may forget your latest slip of the tongue, but your slip of the keyboard may haunt you forever.

I think this digital dichotomy is an effect of viewing the Internet and what you do online as your own private world. You create it, therefore you control it from your own personal point of privacy. But you forget that the Web is worldwide and more porous than a ratty blanket. Whatever happens in Vegas may stay in Vegas, but that slogan could *never* be used for the Internet.

It's just another way the virtual world warps perception of the real one.

About-Face

As tempting as it is to turn away from life and its problems to escape into a virtual reality, it's not helpful. No matter how difficult your real life is, escaping online won't improve it. The Internet may provide an engaging diversion, numb your pain, erase your boredom, or ease your suffering for a while, but it can't transform your life.

Only actively *engaging* in that life can. The time and energy spent running away from your real life could be better spent confronting, dealing with, changing, and bettering that life.

This is true when real life is normal, but it's especially true when real life is hard. When you're under severe stress, your online life may seem to help you cope with your real life, but it only puts off reality. Life is waiting for you as soon as you log off, and sometimes it's worse. Maintaining emotional health in the midst of a difficult situation requires all your attention, strength, and stamina. It requires you to be alert and aware of how real events are affecting you. And it requires seeking real help to change your circumstances instead of retreating into a virtual reality to escape.

Life must be lived about-face and head-on; otherwise you're bound to be blindsided. While you're spending time keeping up with everything online, you'll lose track of your kids. While you're spending all that time with your online friends, you'll become alienated from those closest to you. While you spend all that time hiding from who you are, you'll miss the opportunity to grow and mature as a person. While you spend all that time in a virtual world, the clock is ticking on this temporal one.

CONNECTION SECTION

What has become clear to me is that some people think of themselves as having two different personas—one in real life and one in virtual, or online, life. I'm amazed at how many people like their online persona more than their real-life one. I'm amazed at how many people think they can be more honest online than face-to-face. If that's you, it's no wonder the lure of the Internet and online activities are so strong.

You are not two people. You have just chosen to view yourself that way.

I'd like you to think about how you choose to express yourself online as opposed to how you do so off-line:

Do your conversations off-line mirror how you speak online? Think about the words you use, even the slang words or Internet abbreviations you use. Does your online conversation contain more pithy one-liners than you're able to come up with on the spot in real-time conversations? Do you find yourself funnier online than off? Smarter?

Think about the pictures you post. Do you specifically choose those you consider most flattering? Do you choose pictures that reveal only a part of your face or show you at an odd angle? Take a look at the picture you use to identify yourself when posting. What are you trying to tell others about yourself through that photo? Is it the truth?

What about the way you respond to people online compared to face-to-face? Do you find it easier to respond online in a way you wouldn't be comfortable doing in person or on the phone? Do you find it easier to talk to people or divulge feelings or thoughts online than in person? If so, why do you suppose that is?

Think also here about how you text, not just being online on a computer. Texting also can create a persona.

If your personality only exists online, that persona is ephemeral, evaporating as soon as you log off. You still have to face the real you in the bathroom mirror.

People can become so obsessed with creating, maintaining, and grooming their online personalities they end up taking away that energy from who they really are. You may be able to convince your 130 Facebook friends that everything is great and you don't have any problems. You may be able to put up artful photos of yourself where age and gravity are defied. You may be able to send targeted tweets and texts highlighting your abbreviated brilliance. And you may be able to congratulate yourself at the end of the day with how marvelous, attractive, and urbane you are. But if your personality only exists online, that persona is ephemeral, evaporating as soon as you log off. You still have to face the real you in the bathroom mirror.

The Internet makes a great escape hatch and a place to hide out from the world. But you should ask yourself, "Why am I hiding?" You should ask yourself, "What am I avoiding?" If you're hiding out and trying to avoid yourself, your life, and who you are, it's a myth. There is no place you can go, virtual or otherwise, where *you* are not *there*. And since you actually are with yourself all the time, why not determine to spend that time getting to know, like, accept, and appreciate yourself, or even change yourself for the better?

If you've been using your online presence as a way to mask yourself, commit to greater honesty online—with yourself and others. Begin a process of evaluating what you post. Think before you write. Think before you post. Ask yourself, "What am I trying to say here? Is it honest? Is this the truth?"

Go to your Facebook wall and look with new eyes at the content. Use the same criteria: Is it honest? Is it the truth? Facebook is a canvas you use to paint a picture of yourself to the world. You only have one life, one portrait being created through the passage of time. Facebook should reflect the grand artistry that is your life and who you truly are, not an imaginary, artificial caricature.

Real life is ultimately far more compelling than the chimera of a virtual life.

Think back to some of the most compelling photographs you've ever seen of people that touched your heart and made an impression. Were they of perfectly posed people, with painted smiles and brilliantly white teeth? Or were they of real people whose faces reflected the truth of their lives, their real lives, in that moment—from pain to compassion to purpose to exultation? There is something compelling about seeing someone express real life in truth. Real life is ultimately far more compelling than the chimera of a virtual life.

Chapter 6

REAL CONNECTION

JULIE FELT CONFLICTED. Deep inside she heard a small voice warning her what she was doing didn't seem right. Another voice, however, insisted there was nothing wrong. At the moment she was listening to the second voice and telling the first to pipe down. She couldn't be doing anything wrong; she was merely typing, for heaven's sake! It wasn't like they were even in the same state. He lived in Wisconsin; she lived in Colorado. And it wasn't like she'd gone looking for him after all these years. He was just there one day as she was reconnecting with old college buds. They were both married with kids; she'd seen his pictures and he'd seen hers. It was all in the open, right? There was nothing to feel guilty about or blow out of proportion.

So why didn't the first little voice shut up?

Maybe the first voice had marked the thrill she'd felt upon

reconnecting. It brought back a rush of emotion and an odd sort of joy, like finding something precious you didn't know you'd lost. He hadn't changed a bit: no one could make her laugh more quickly. His posts were hysterical and made her feel twenty years younger and twenty pounds lighter; he made Julie feel like *herself* again, the way she'd been back in the day—before career and marriage and kids and all that. "Don't get me wrong," she lectured the first voice, "I'm not trying to go back there. I wouldn't change my life." It's just that, well, Scotty reminded her of a part of herself she hadn't realized she'd misplaced over the years. Julie rationalized that keeping contact wasn't about Scotty so much as it was about her. It was her personal rediscovery, and it made her feel good.

Plus, there was nothing remotely sexual about their conversations. Neither of them had expressed anything more than tidbits and commentaries about their lives, their spouses, their families, and their jobs. It was all very innocent. Without meaning to, Julie remembered having a dream the other night about Scotty. Just one of those I-wonder-what dreams you sometimes have about other people. She didn't remember most of the details, just that Scotty had been in it and Casey had not. That didn't mean anything, though; Casey wasn't in all her dreams. It was just one of those weird random dreams that don't make a lot of sense and you barely remember. One dream didn't mean anything.

Shaking off that first voice, Julie continued to type, relating a quirky thing that happened at work. She couldn't wait to get Scotty's reaction. Luckily she never had to wait long because Scotty seemed to be on Facebook a lot and was usually quick to get back to her. Once there was a three-day lag, and she'd remarked about it. He wrote back about a weekend visit to the in-laws—a truly delicious post with all the gory details! Now if he was going to be away from the keyboard for a while, he let her know so she wouldn't worry. That was just being considerate, her second voice said, drowning out the first.

Often the people we disconnect from are the ones closest to us because they're the ones who know the truth.

DISCONNECTED

In the last chapter we talked about the virtual world people can create online, as well as the false sense of anonymity many feel about their online activities. These create an atmosphere of separateness. This atmosphere can disconnect us from others in our lives. People don't usually create spouse and children avatars. They don't enter virtual worlds with virtual minivans and car seats. In an odd way, the draw of online activities can be as much about *dis*connecting as it is connecting. And often the people we disconnect from are the ones closest to us because they're the ones who know the truth; they're the first responders who point out the disparity between the real us and the virtual us. If our goal is cruise the cyber-highway on an escape from reality, the last thing we want is a family road trip, like the one last summer to Aunt Martha's in Kansas. That one took way too long, with too many people in the car, and had more than enough "reality" to last for several years. Cyber-highway trips are fast, lean, and definitely unencumbered.

Every person has problems, so relationships are problems multiplied. Like a perverse algebraic equation, when Jack is in relationship with Jill, Jack's problems become intertwined with Jill's and vice versa. Now each person has multiple problems. Start adding jobs, debt, kids, parents, siblings, and extended family into the mix, and now you're talking geometric progression. In contrast your online life can be a singular one. Sure, you can talk about your spouse, your kids, or your family, but you do so at your discretion. If you want to pretend for fifteen minutes they don't exist, you can. A real-life disappointed spouse can be difficult to ignore, but online you don't even have to acknowledge you're married. A real-life defiant teenager is difficult to avoid; online you can just keep his sixth grade photo up indefinitely.

Your virtual life must be created; your real life must be lived. You have creative authority over the one; you have limited control over the other. Adulthood and maturity are all about navigating a way through that balance between the authority you want and the control you actually have. In a way, a virtual world can be like remaining in an adolescent state; it actually can be all about you, and only you, 24/7 if you choose. Like a teenager, it can be attractive to live in the illusion of control. Most teenagers flirt with independence while knowing they remain

---

Beyond 140 Bytes

Sometimes people make connections, solve problems, and encounter delight using social media, but their stories don't get exposed. Twitter hopes to change that with Stories .Twitter.com.

Here's a selection of headlines featured on the front page shortly after launch:[1]

- Aaron Durand...saved his mom's bookstore with a tweet
- Roger Ebert...gained a new voice after losing his ability to speak
- Queen Rania al Abdualla...started a global conversation (with a sandwich)
- Bullet Skan...found safety when the revolution in Tunisia reached his backyard

supported by their parents. Similarly you can flirt with independence online while knowing you remain connected to your off-line relationships. Like teenagers who tend to take their parents for granted, when you live online you can begin to take your off-line relationships for granted.

VIRTUAL INTIMACY

Because online relationships occur in the virtual world and not the real one, they can take on an unreal nature. They can fast-forward into deep, personal areas more quickly through the written word than they ever would through the spoken word. It can be much easier to divulge your secrets when you're looking at a bitmap than when you're looking at a person.

Like teenagers who tend to take their parents for granted, when you live online you can begin to take your off-line relationships for granted.

In my previous book *Hidden Dangers of the Internet*, I said that online activities provide a powerful mix of immediacy, anonymity, and intimacy and that this combination has the potential to catch a person unprepared for its potency. This is especially true when dealing with sexual content, whether visual or written. We've talked about how fast and immediate things are online: if you want it, you can find it. We've also talked about the aura of anonymity the Internet still has: only you and your ISP need ever know. Now I'd like to talk about the shortcuts to intimacy that can be found online.

In our sex-obsessed culture we tend to view intimacy as merely physical, to narrow its focus to sexual activity. But this is not an accurate picture of the power of intimacy to create and forge personal relationships. There is more to intimacy than physical contact. Intimacy also speaks to a sense of closeness, familiarity, of knowing someone, of an attachment to another person. It is ironic that we often equate intimacy with sex when sexual contact is often amazingly casual with little real closeness, familiarity, or true attachment formed. As a culture we don't understand real intimacy at all. Online activities, especially Facebook, are providing proof that a sense of intimacy and betrayal of intimacy don't require sex at all, much less physical contact.

As I've worked with married couples where one or both spouses have cheated on the other, it's become clear to me that sex is rarely the primary force driving an affair. The void filled by illicit sex is emotional, not physical. It happens when a connection forms outside of the marriage that begins to satisfy and validate unmet emotional needs. When deep emotional needs are filled outside the marriage relationship, the result is a type of emotional adultery. What begins as emotional adultery can then turn into physical adultery (though not always). Whether or not physical adultery follows, emotional adultery is still a violation of the marital relationship because it fractures the relational unity marriage was designed to provide.

Online communication seems to me to pose a threat of emotional adultery to relationships—and I'm speaking here mainly about the marriage relationship. I believe these online relationships are potentially threatening because online relationships are based largely on ideas, thoughts, and feelings—the foundation of emotional life. Sure, some people just post and communicate what they do on a daily basis, but that gets boring pretty quickly and doesn't form an emotional connection: "Got up." "Went to Starbucks." "Had a meeting at work." "Pasta for lunch." "Drove home in traffic."

"Fed the cat." "Watched *American Idol*." Factual? Yes. Intimate, interesting, and engaging? No. The intriguing aspect of online communication is not necessarily the *what* of peoples' lives but the *why*—how they feel about their life and what they're doing, the thoughts and ideas they express and are passionate about. These are windows into the soul and, as such, can be compelling. This is the essence of the emotional connection that can occur in online relationships.

Whether or not physical adultery follows, emotional adultery is still a violation of the marital relationship because it fractures the relational unity marriage was designed to provide.

If you spend more time and energy explaining who you are online than you do in person, you're going to have a problem with your real-life relationships. Real-life relationships and the communication surrounding them can become more about taking out the garbage, figuring out who's going to drop the kids off at soccer, filling out the grocery list, or any number of the minutia, flotsam, and jetsam of life. These are the nuts and bolts of everyday activities, but there's nothing sexy, special, or revelatory about them.

Juxtapose that with an online relationship where you're exposing your innermost thoughts, expressing your deeply held beliefs, and trading witty, substantive, emotional content. This person becomes your adult pen pal, your sounding board, your confidante. Online you're genuinely asked how you feel about events of the day; offline you're distractedly asked if you picked up the dry cleaning. In an odd twist this virtual relationship can become the platform through which you begin to reveal the real you. When this happens, you disconnect from your real-life relationship and reattach to your online one. This is emotional adultery.

GREENER GRASS

Envision a couple standing in a corner at church talking about another couple they haven't seen for months, who they just discovered are getting a divorce. In hushed tones they both think back over what they know and remember about the troubled couple. He comments how they seemed to be unhappy and sometimes didn't even sit together. She remarks she couldn't remember the two of them ever holding hands or putting an arm around each other or ever showing any physical closeness. Together they decide how sad the news is and determine "they just drifted apart."

Life isn't static, and disconnected things have a tendency to drift. When you're adrift in your marriage, it is so much easier to connect to someone online. And if that happens, it's even easier to continue disconnecting from your marriage. Now the online relationship that previously satisfied only your emotional needs becomes a conduit through which to consider addressing your physical needs. The need sparks a fantasy that begets reality. This is why there are stories of a husband or wife leaving their spouse and moving across country to consummate an old relationship that reignited on Facebook. The online relationship becomes the "greener grass" in that old saying "The grass is always greener on the other side."

The greener-grass scenario is an interesting one. In it you're never responsible for the sad state of affairs on your side of the fence. But that's not true in real life. For those couples whose marriages were in shambles because of emotional adultery, I often wonder what would have happened if all that time, effort, and energy that was sunk into the other relationship had been invested into the marriage instead? Maybe the reason the grass is in such poor condition on this side is because you've been neglecting to water, feed, and care for it.

Watering, feeding, and weeding your lawn take a lot of time and effort. Every year I'm reminded of that fact as I wage a continuing battle against the moss that flourishes during our wet Pacific Northwest winters. Your real-life relationships are no different: they take time and energy and often require you to do nitpicky stuff like weeding out misunderstandings and resentments and working out the delegation of chores and responsibilities. Online relationships can be like Astroturf: from a distance and in poor lighting they look alike, but one is artificial. It may look greener, but it's not truly alive.

The greener-grass scenario is an interesting one. In it you're never responsible for the sad state of affairs on your side of the fence.

A Site for Sore Eyes

Of course, not everyone is married, nor does everyone want to be. But many would like to be, or at least they want a long-term committed relationship. So how do you go about finding that someone special? It used to be you went to singles' events or establishments, or you might get paired up by family, friends, or coworkers. It was a crapshoot with lousy odds, considering the amount of time, energy, and effort expended compared with the number of people with whom you came into contact.

Enter the Internet. According to Consumer-Rakings.com, the top five dating sites are:[2]

- Match.com, with 29 million singles and a guarantee you'll meet someone "special" within six months[3]

- Chemistry.com, with 4 million singles and "relationship advice from recognized experts"[4]

- PerfectMatch.com, with 4 million active profiles and "convenient e-mail notifications about potential matches"[5]

- eHarmony.com, with over 20 million members, designed to create long-lasting relationships"[6]

- Spark.com, with 1 million singles and an "ability to send profiles to friends"[7]

There are dating sites for Christians, for Catholics, for Jews, for seniors, for single parents, for casual daters. I could have done more research into smaller niche dating sites, but there are some places on the Internet I'd rather not visit: dating sites are notorious for hosting frankly pornographic content. Several major sites (including one targeting Christians, BigChurch, and another targeting Jews, JewishFriendFinder) are owned by the former Penthouse Media Group, now known as FriendFinder Networks.[8] Be careful.

The world of dating has changed and will change even more in response to the power of the Internet. If you are single and are looking to enter the world of Internet dating, I have a few suggestions:

- *Jettison any Cinderella or Prince Charming syndromes.* Internet profiles are most often designed to present someone in a favorable, air-brushed light. After all, isn't that sort of what you tried to do when you created yours? Keep a tight grip on reality as you read through the profiles of others, remembering the time-tested advice *if it looks too good to be true, it probably is.*

There Is No Third Base Online

Anthropologist and zoologist Desmond Morris has observed that healthy human sexual intimacy normally follows a twelve-stage process that progresses from casual intimacy, requiring little trust, to sexual intimacy, requiring a great deal of trust. When the normal pattern of intimacy is rushed, or when stages are skipped, the relationship can be "fraught with danger"—the two partners may bond for a time, due to cultural pressures, but will be vulnerable to bonding with someone else. "The couple's natural potential for falling in love still lies waiting inside their brains and can leap into action without warning at any time, to create a true bond somewhere outside their official one."[9]

Not only are modern pressures and cultural changes causing many to rush the natural progression of trust and intimacy, but also the advent of Internet-mediated communication tools are making it easier and easier to completely bypass *all* the physical stages of intimacy, leading many to become susceptible to online relationships that culminate in real-world affairs.

Here are the stages of physical intimacy as identified by Morris:[10]

1. Eye to body
2. Eye to eye
3. Voice to voice
4. Hand to hand
5. Arm to shoulder
6. Arm to waist
7. Mouth to mouth
8. Hand to head
9. Hand to body
10. Mouth to breast
11. Hand to genitals
12. Genitals to genitals

- *Honesty is the best policy.* Don't try to hide who you are. Be honest and open. Deception is a terrible foundation upon which to build a relationship. Use current, up-to-date pictures, not from the wedding five years ago that miraculously made you look three inches taller and ten pounds thinner.

- *Do your homework.* Thoroughly check out different sites you're considering. Look at the overall presentation on the site, the graphics used, the pictures used, and the general tone. If you already feel uncomfortable viewing the homepage, it's not the site for you; try another.

- *Don't compromise your principles.* Choose a dating site that reflects your values and then stick to them throughout the entire process, from signing up to creating your profile to evaluating the profiles of others to entering into relationships.

- *Don't panic.* You're not buying a used car that could drive off the lot before you get there. Relationships take time to recognize, initiate, and cultivate. Relax and take your time.

- *Follow your gut.* Be aware of your reactions and feelings as you go through the process. It's incredible how much communication is subliminal. Call it wisdom, intuition, a sixth sense, or your conscience—but pay attention.

- *Do your own work first.* If you're not comfortable with yourself, how can you expect anyone else to be?

Relationships with other people should not be used merely as a distraction from your relationship with yourself. Learn to like, love, appreciate, and value yourself first, and you'll be better equipped to extend those blessings to someone else.

• *Check yourself for ulterior motives.* What are you honestly looking for? Is this about putting yourself out there and finding that someone special, or is this about an internally focused voyeuristic excuse to mine the photos, intimate details, and lives of other people? The ultimate point of a dating site should be to meet real people, not spend all of your time with online profiles.

The ultimate point of a dating site should be to meet real people, not spend all of your time with online profiles.

Anecdotally, I've heard from friends and acquaintances that dating sites are a mixed bag. Some friends have found great relationships that way, and others have tried it only to find that special someone the old-fashioned way—the cousin of a friend of a coworker or some other complicated but somewhat normal connection point. Still others have gone through a host of profiles only to be disappointed every time. Dating sites are not panaceas; they're just another way to begin to make connections with other people. I applaud the effort to try to find that special someone, being happily married myself. Go online, sure, but remember to bring your honesty, integrity, values, and principles with you when you go.

Connecting a search for love, romance, and intimacy with the Internet needs to be done alertly, maturely, and cautiously.

ARTIFICIAL INTIMACY

A chapter on relationships online would be deficient without discussing the power and addictive nature of pornography online. I wish I could say I see less and less of this in my practice, but I cannot. Internet pornography is a serious issue for many people, mostly men, but increasingly for women too.[11]

In a 2004 *Wired* magazine article about Senate hearings on Internet pornography, Mary Anne Layden, codirector of the Sexual Trauma and Psychopathology Program at the University of Pennsylvania's Center for Cognitive Therapy, described pornography as the "most concerning thing to psychological health that I know of existing today." She went on to say, "The Internet is a perfect drug delivery system because you are anonymous, aroused and have role models for these behaviors."[12]

Emotional adultery devastates relationships because it unhinges emotional attachment and reconnects it online. Pornography devastates relationships because it overwhelms and hijacks sexual fulfillment. The use of pornography for sexual outlet constitutes a betrayal to basic family relationships as it takes one of the fundamental blessings of marriage—the physical act of sex—and turns it inward, perverting it into an autoerotic expression. Online pornography is one more way the Internet can become all about you—what you want, when you want it, how you want it—to the exclusion of your primary relationships. As Layden said, the Internet is the perfect delivery system for the drug of pornography and explicit sexual content.

"The Internet is a perfect drug delivery system because you are anonymous, aroused, and have role models for these behaviors." —Mary Anne Layden

---

Here are some statistics on Internet pornography (like all Internet statistics, these are subject to change, given the fluid nature of the Web):[13]

- Twelve percent of websites are pornographic—nearly 25 million sites.

- Forty million Americans regularly visit porn sites.

- Of those 40 million, a third are women.

- Seventy percent of males, ages eighteen to twenty-four, monthly visit porn sites.

- Eight percent of all e-mails have pornographic content.

- Thirty-four percent of Internet users report receiving unwanted pornographic content through pop-up ads, misdirected links, or unwanted e-mails.

- Every day there are 116,000 searches for "child pornography."

- The average age when a child is exposed to Internet pornography is eleven years of age.

- The least popular day in the United States for viewing porn is Thanksgiving.

- The most popular day in the United States for viewing porn is Sunday.

The prevalence and use of pornography is not decreasing; it's increasing and sweeping up many good men and women into its virtual vortex. There are professionals all over the world whose daily, hourly, primary goal is to get you to view pornography. They are making billions and billions of dollars every year. These porn hustlers know that for a percentage of you, if they can get you to view pornography once, they can get you to view it again.

The use of pornography, as an addiction, is not static. It is progressive in nature. The compulsion to use it to achieve sexual gratification does not lessen over time; it increases. The content does not improve over time; it deteriorates. The shame does not numb over time; it sears. Pornography will say yes to every base thought, every disgusting desire. It does not judge; it merely provides. Pornography says yes to every sexual desire, and the Internet is able to accommodate. What is illegal in this country does not operate under the same "restriction" in other countries with pornography's global reach. It is not merely the number and breadth of pornographic images available; as graphics and animation become more and more sophisticated, the ability to create sexual avatars increases.

These porn hustlers know that for a percentage of you, if they can get you to view pornography once, they can get you to view it again.

Graphic, visual pornography is a real temptation that must be acknowledged and factored, but you need to be aware that pornography can also be written. *Merriam-Webster's* defines *pornography* as "the depiction of erotic behavior (as in pictures or writing) intended to cause sexual excitement."[14] Written pornography isn't confined merely to the pages of romance novels and adult magazines. Written pornography need not be produced only by those using pseudonyms. If you engage in sexually explicit written content with another person for the purpose of causing either your own or the other's sexual excitement, you could be engaging in pornography.

Sexual excitement and gratification have a God-given purpose and place. Trust me when I say the Internet and online relationships are not that purpose and not that place. Pornography is addictive and progressive, and the mind can hold those images, unlike chemical substances that can be detoxed out of the body, indefinitely. Sexual desire is a powerful component of our lives as human beings. It is unwise to weld that power to something as powerfully compelling as the Internet. In a contest of sheer will, this is not a fight you're guaranteed to win.

If this is an area of concern for you or someone you know, I urge you to seek professional help. You can contact us at The Center by going to our website at APlaceOfHope.com or seek resources in your local area. Whatever you do, don't pretend it isn't a problem or delude yourself into thinking you can deal with it alone. You got into this state alone; now you need help getting out. Your best avenue for success in overcoming a pornographic or sexual addiction is by working with a trained professional therapist.

Tend Your Relationships

Earlier I said that people were problems and relationships were problems multiplied. That's certainly true, but that's only one side of the story; it's the side of the story that looks at the grass on your side and sees only moss and weeds. There is no such thing as a perfect lawn, no matter how hard you work at it. Lawns, like relationships, are growing things, so they move and change and grow; lawns, like relationships, need tending. When you spend all of your time tending your online relationships, you have no time to nurture your real-life relationships. Give all your water, food, and care to your virtual relationships, and you'll watch your real-life ones suffer and wither.

Your family and friends need honest connection, not 140-character generic Christmas-letter sound bites.

Spouses need time to talk to you—and not just about mundane duties and family responsibilities. They need to hear you articulate your inner feelings, your dreams, your hopes, and your passions—even if you've been married for decades. Children need more than directives; they need discussion. They need to hear about how you live your life and why, what's important to you, and what things you would change. Most of all, they need to know they are important, more important than viral videos, e-mail, Facebook, or texting, even if they don't always reciprocate that importance well. Extended family and friends need more than just the leftover slots in your week or month. Your family and friends need honest connection, not 140-character generic Christmas-letter sound bites. All of these take time and patience, along with physical and emotional presence. Are there other relationships to be had, explored, and cultivated on the Internet? Sure, but you must prioritize your existing family commitments over any online activities.

FACEBOOK AND YOUR MARRIAGE

For you who are married and who absolutely love social networking, I'd like to recommend a delightful book called

Facebook and Your Marriage by K. Jason and Kelli Krafsky (see FacebookAndYourMarriage.com). This visually engaging and smartly written book can help you determine how to integrate positive relationship strategies into your Facebook use.

Facebook is not going away, and if you're going to use it to further your relationships, you might as well make the primary relationship you improve and cultivate your own marriage!

CONNECTION SECTION

Some people are hooked because of the technology itself, and some people are hooked because technology becomes a conduit through which they meet their emotional needs. Truly, the delivery system doesn't matter. A few years ago it was e-mail and chatrooms; now it's Facebook. A couple years ago it was talking on the phone; now it's texting. Before, it was all about blogging; now it's tweeting.

For this Connection Section I'd like you to focus not on the technology itself but on what you personally get out of the technology. Think about the following questions:

- What are you doing online?

- How are you connecting to others?

- What is the content of that connection?

- Would you be willing for your spouse or members of your family to view all of your online activities and content?

- Relationships are formed through time—what relationships do you have online?

- What emotional needs are being met through these online relationships?

- How would you feel if you were unable to connect online for a day? A week? A month?

- How many nonfamily online relationships do you maintain?

- Of those relationships, how many do you keep strictly online—meaning you don't talk or visit but only connect online?

- As you evaluate the content of your online relationships or activities, are there any that pose a threat or provide competition to your real-life relationships?

- Are you willing, within the next week, to modify, limit, or sever any online relationship or activity that poses such a threat?

- If so, what is your step-by-step action plan for doing that?

- If you're not willing, what is holding you back? Be specific. Are you willing to seek professional help to overcome this barrier?

- Do you have a need to view pornographic content?

- Have you felt ashamed about your online pornographic use and tried to stop?

- What things do you tell yourself when you want to stop so that you can continue?

- What is the truth?

Swiss novelist and playwright Max Frisch once said, "Technology [is] the knack of so arranging the world that we don't have to experience it."[15] Life cannot be arranged; it must be experienced. Life needs to be accepted and lived out in truth. The grass may appear greener on the Internet, but it is virtual turf. It's arranged; it isn't real. People don't always sally with perfect 140-bite rejoinders in real life. People post pictures and upload videos and create content that isn't complete and isn't fully accurate. Written thoughts and feelings are low-bandwidth and don't come with visual and audible context; you don't get to see the look in the eye, the tilt of the head. You don't get to hear the tone of voice, the snort, or the sigh. Even the most transparent of us have blind sides and unwitting opacity.

Real connection is best conducted in real life.

"Technology [is] the knack of so arranging the world that we don't have to experience it." —Max Frisch

---

Chapter 7

INSTANT DOWNLOAD

KEVIN COULD FEEL his blood pressure climbing, which wouldn't make his doctor happy, but that's what the meds were for. He was already running behind, and now some idiot had decided that 2:42 p.m. on a workday was a great time for road repair. Looking around, he tried to decide if it was worth checking e-mail on his iPhone. It was tempting, but fines were double in construction zones, and Kevin was already worried that last month's speeding ticket was about to catch up to his insurance. That ticket might put him over the edge, so, as much as he resented it, he had to be good. Surely this backup couldn't be that much longer.

His hands-free meant he'd already checked voice mail, but nobody at work ever used that; everything was either e-mail or text: much faster. Oh, look—he was up to twenty-seven miles an hour, at least for a little ways. Up ahead: more brake lights. Perfect. What a monumental waste of time! The number of things he should be doing besides being stuck behind a battered Isuzu pickup was endless. He could feel all of that time draining uselessly away.

The longer Kevin spent crawling down the freeway, the angrier he grew. The nonstop mental venting rendered the sports radio channel into so much meaningless background chatter. Checking the dashboard clock and calibrating his location, he figured he was going to be at least seven or eight minutes late. Forget the ticket, he decided, as he started bobbing his eyes up toward the roadway and then down to his phone, sending a quick text that he was stuck in traffic. Kevin hated being late, although it happened routinely.

The worst thing was he couldn't possibly make up the time. It was gone, irretrievable. Not only was he going to be late to his own meeting, but he would now be solidly behind for the entire rest of the day. Fuming, he felt trapped by circumstances and stymied by time. The only thing accelerating at this point was his blood pressure.

As a society, our perception of time and the good, of what is instant and what is slow, has changed.

Time Warped

For several years I've been intrigued by my own perception of time. Part of it is age-related, I'm sure: the older I get, the more time seems to rocket into the future. The harder I try to catch up, the farther it seems out of reach. It's age and kids and my particular time of life—but I don't think that's all it is. Part of this feeling that I'm never caught up, that I'm always behind, is cultural. As a society, our perception of time and the good, of what is instant and what is slow, has changed.

It used to be that the generations differentiated themselves through how much physical effort was required to provide for themselves and their families. Whenever younger generations complained about some perceived hardship, the older generation gave admonitions like, "I used to walk two miles in the snow just to get to school." Or you heard, "When I was your age, I used to haul hay bales from sunup to sundown," as a way to put an end to whining over having to engage in anything physical that didn't involve a sports team. Then technology advances shifted the scope and breadth of physical labor. Over the last half of the past century labor and manufacturing jobs shifted into information, technology, and service jobs. Technology fueled the change as machinery was conceived, constructed, and utilized to replace physical effort. A discontinuity developed between what different generations thought of as "a hard day's work" or how each defined a "hardship."

Now technology has caused yet another similar generational shift. Today, though, it's not about effort; it's about time. Instead of a difference between how physical work or effort is perceived between generations, the shift in the perception of time is perceived due to advances and innovations in technology. We have entered into a new sort of time warp.

Our *expectations* about time have become warped. Our culture drives the need for speed, and the need for speed drives our culture. Technology fuels this circular momentum. We demand speed from technology, and when it delivers, it alters our perception of fast and slow and what is good or bad about each. It alters our concept of patience, endurance, and perseverance; it alters our perception of what is acceptable and what is unacceptable. The benchmarks have been moved; in fact, the benchmarks themselves are moving at a very fast pace, and our perceptions can barely keep up.

Today's equivalent of the "walking miles in the snow" complaint is now "we used to have to wait on a dial-up modem." I already talked about how strange it must be to this youngest generation that you had to wait to make a phone call until you found a phone because you didn't happen to carry one around in your back pocket. You even had to wait to find a phone book just to know where to go. You had to wait to get to a place where the information waited because you didn't

Moore's Law

Have you ever wondered why the pace of change seems to be getting faster and faster while devices get smaller and smaller? It's no accident.

In 1965 Intel cofounder Gordon E. Moore noticed that the number of components used on integrated circuit boards had doubled every year from 1958 to 1965. He speculated this trend would continue for at least another ten years.

Today his prediction still seems to hold true, only it's not so much a prediction anymore: it is a law, a rule of thumb guiding business strategy and high-tech decision-making. It's not just that *it so happens* that we cram more stuff onto smaller chips every couple of years: tech manufacturers use this "law" to guide their long-term planning and R&D (research and development) targets.

While Moore was describing the physical complexity of computer circuit boards, one of his colleagues at Intel, David House, went even further with Moore's impromptu law. He predicted that not only would *complexity* double, but also that *performance* would double as well.

Doomsday futurists (or utopians, depending on their view) now speculate that at some point in the not-too-distant future, all this exponential doubling in performance and halving in size will result in a "technological singularity," a period where "progress in technology occurs almost instantly."[1]

If you think your technology expectations are high now, just wait.

carry around a device that brought information to you. The startling, disturbing constant in all those scenarios is "you had to wait." You had to take time. It was slow. The perceived hardship is not getting what you wanted as fast as you can get it now. How did we ever survive?

We survived slowly. And it was good.

GREAT EXPECTATIONS

Technology has altered our expectations, and expectations have a huge impact on our lives, our happiness, our sense of security, and our ability to live a balanced, peaceful life. Unfulfilled expectations fuel negatively charged emotions such as anger, annoyance, frustration, irritation, and dissatisfaction. When you move the bar of expectations, you move the bar of fulfillment and satisfaction. As Pat Morley has often put it, "All disappointment is the result of unmet expectations."[2] With technology, the bar of expectations isn't being moved as much as dragged ever forward.

I now routinely expect the instantaneous, the near miraculous, all as a mundane part of my day.

When I got my first computer, over twenty years ago, I was so enamored and thrilled with all it could do. It was a 386 with an MS-DOS operating system and a dial-up modem. The hard drive was big, the fan was loud, and the monitor rivaled a vacuum-tube television in size. I used to start it and go get a sandwich or make a phone call while it booted up. I didn't panic or become angry as it took several minutes to do what was, back then, amazing. I had a different expectation. My blood pressure didn't spike and I didn't mentally revert to using a sailor's vocabulary. I was calm, happy, and appreciative of all the things it could do.

Then technology moved my expectations.

I now routinely expect the instantaneous, the near miraculous, all as a mundane part of my day. I expect there to be zero issues when I log in to my computer. I expect to have full bars on my cell phone. I expect to log in to my favorite websites without a hitch. When this doesn't happen, I can feel anxious, resentful, and angry. All of this stuff is supposed to work when I want and how I want. And quickly. After all, I pay for it. After all, I'm in control.

CONTROL ISSUE

In this culture, being in control of time means being in control of life. We come to rely on it. When we don't get what we've come to rely on, we get angry. Our internal sense of fairness and the way the world ought to be gets thwacked out of joint. We become hypersensitive to the slightest irritation. We feel we're being unfairly targeted, as if the whole world was somehow set against us. We feel besieged; under attack, we react defensively. Since it's only marginally satisfying to yell at a yellow light, a slow Internet connection, or a dead cell zone, we transfer that negative energy to the people around us. The cliché scenario used to be when a man got reprimanded at work, he went home and argued with his wife, who then yelled at the child, who subsequently kicked the dog, who finally chased the cat. Now this whole negative cycle can get started simply because of something as fluid and chaotic as our expectations over time. We become stressed out over our expectations of what we need to get done or should have already gotten done and how fast we think all of that should happen. Our sense of peace and calm has devolved into a panic by an altered perception of time. It's amazing how quickly this accelerated pace becomes the new normal.

Can I text you halfway around the country in thirty seconds? Yes. It's easy; it's quick. With a few clicks I have taken the initiative and shot the ball back into your court. Because it was so quick and easy for me to send the text, I now have an expectation that it is going to be quick and easy for you to return the text. And so I wait. But you don't text back. Why not? It's fast and easy and, what, I'm not worth thirty seconds of your time and attention today? How hard can it be to just punch in a couple of keystrokes and respond to my text? The longer it takes you to respond, the more irritated I get. I have instant access to your *cell phone* through technology, and, in my mind, it means I should have instant access to *you*. This is my expectation, and because you have not met it, I am left to stew in my unfulfilled expectation.

If we didn't have cell phones or the ability to send a text message, I wouldn't have such expectations. Thirty years ago I would have called your landline, and if you didn't answer, it meant you forgot to turn on your tape-driven answering machine (again!) and I'd just have to try a different time. Twenty years ago I would have called your landline and at least have gotten your always-on voice mail so I could leave a message, but I'd still have to wait for you to call me back. Now you have a cell phone, and you should keep it with you at all times on the off chance, on any given day, for any given reason, I should want to get hold of you and send you a text. And now with services like Google Voice, even if I slow down enough to actually call you, and even if you don't answer the three phones that ring simultaneously (home, office, *and* cell), when I do finally leave my irritated voicemail, Google transcribes it automatically and forwards the text along with an audio file to your e-mail account of choice. You cannot escape my urgency. And I'm still waiting.

Think about going to see a movie. It used to be you had to get into your car, drive to the theater, wait in line for the ticket, wait in another line for your popcorn and candy, watch all of the local advertisers' slideshows, endure the trailers and coming attractions, and then, and only then, you finally got to your movie. Now you can watch it within a minute by downloading it to your Xbox, catching it on NetFlix or Hulu with your iPad, or ordering it via OnDemand. What a happy concept—OnDemand. Getting what you want *on demand* is near kinglike power and control. Does it cost you a few bucks on your cable bill? Does it come out of your queue on Netflix? Yes, but isn't instant gratification worth at least five bucks? And don't you wish everything in life was so quick, easy, and controllable?

How much is instant relief worth? Our lives are filled with tasks, duties, and obligations. Each unfulfilled burden creates tension— internal tension (When am I going to get that done?), external tension (When is he going to get that done?), or both. A task, duty, or obligation is like a ball we've thrown up into the air; at some point we're going to have to catch it or let it fall. The question of which will happen produces tension. And the more balls you have in the air? More tension.

Getting what you want on demand is near kinglike power and control.

Technology promises to help us manage the tension by helping us juggle all those balls in the air. (As we talked about in chapter 2, "Multi-Taxed," it also causes the air balls to multiply, but we've decided that's an acceptable price to pay.) With cell phones, tablets, and computers I can get relief from tasks, duties, and obligations at 1:00 a.m., while driving to work, while waiting in line at the grocery store, or while sitting on the sidelines of a soccer game (more on that in a bit).

TYRANNY OF THE URGENT

There is a cultural conversation going on now about the amazingly impolite behavior of teenagers, who will drop just about everything (including the steering wheel) to take a call or pick up a text. Sam and Nancy look on in disbelief as Chelsea takes Nathan's call during dinner and proceeds to get up from the table, turning her back on the rest of the family, walking off and attending to whatever it is Nathan wants. Sam and Nancy throw their hands up in the air and ask each other, "What are we? Chopped liver?" For teenagers, peers have precedence, and peers are now primarily connected via technology. So parents are actually paying for those devices that now routinely allow their teenagers to completely disregard, disrespect, and ignore them. Welcome to adolescence. Parents may be important, but peers are categorically and firmly established in teendom under "Urgent."

Before parents throw up their hands and point to their teens in horror, however, they first ought to look at themselves. If parents want to engage their teens in a conversation about family, behavior, and boundaries, they need to be careful, because this is a discussion that can go both ways. Technology has certainly helped teenagers connect to those they have placed in their urgent category. It has also affected how parents respond and react to those things that are in an adult's urgent category. It used to be for parents and adults that any work not completed during what was called the "workday" was either left to be done tomorrow or taken home to complete after dinner and the kids went to bed. Once you left the intercom at work, no one could get hold of you unless they called your home phone, which was considered highly inappropriate unless you were in a medical or safety field. There was such a thing as "family time," and it was generally held sacrosanct. Not so much anymore.

Technology has increased the ways people can be connected, and it's no surprise that the connection points have blurred the lines between work and family, public and private. In the movie *The Devil Wears Prada*, Meryl Streep plays a controlling, no-boundaries boss who retains an umbilical cord connection to her harried assistant, played by Anne Hathaway, via cell phone. The constant all-hours, no-holds-barred demands on the assistant threaten to destroy her

Things Change

Elyse Kaner recently took stock of all the changes wrought by technology. After pondering the "good ole days," she noted some of the more frustrating signs of change. Here are a few items from her list that might resonate with you too![3]

"I remember BC [before computers], when an Apple was something that you ate, the forbidden fruit that got Eve into so much trouble. When a Dell was a place where a farmer could be found and a Mac was a truck with souped-up power."

"When a cloud was a descriptive term for toilet paper, a tweet was what birds did and atwitter was all aflutter."

"I remember when a stream referred to a body of water, fishing was for, well… fish, and trash was what people took out."

"I remember when security was as easy as bolting your back door and storage was a sacred and coveted space reserved for your seldom-used stuff."

"When a nook was akin to a cranny and kindle meant to start a fire."

"When a flash drive was a player streaking a football field and the word 'geek' simply meant uncool. Nerdish. No more. The geeks today are the gods of Technopolis."

relationships until she frees herself by leaving the job. In the movie Hathaway's character has to decide between what is urgent and what is important. Her job is urgent, but her life and relationships are important—more important. She almost forgets this until about the last fifteen minutes of the movie.

Technology has increased the ways people can be connected, and it's no surprise that the connection points have blurred the lines between work and family, public and private.

Technology is very good at projecting the urgent, complete with vibration, warning sounds, growls, special rings, pop-ups, and timely reminders in monthly, weekly, hourly, and minute-by-minute increments. The sheer volume of the urgency can translate into importance.

Back to the sidelines at that soccer game—I can be standing there, cheering my oldest son when a call comes in, and before I know it, just when my son looks over to make sure I've seen his spectacular lateral pass, I've turned away, with my back to the field, trying to relieve just a little bit of my task-duty-obligation tension by taking the call. I've just done the same thing Chelsea did to Sam and Nancy. In her moment Chelsea conveyed to the family that Nathan was more important. In my moment I've conveyed to my son that whatever the phone call is about is more important.

Technology can have this effect on us all. We find ourselves taking calls from some people and, by necessity, ignoring other people. We just find it more annoying when we're the recipients and not the instigators of the behavior.

DISCOMFORT

Why do we do that to each other? Why do we choose to respond to the urgent at the expense of the important? Often it's because the urgent is more annoying and uncomfortable than the important. The urgent is the squeaky brakes, the blinking idiot light on your dashboard, the in-your-face pop-up. It's the loudest noise, the brightest light. We react to the urgent while we put off responding to the important. Important things can be like glaciers; they are inexorable, ever moving but at a slower pace. Important things can build up immense momentum, but they do so over time. It can be tremendously tempting to dart in and out of the path of the important in order to attend to the urgent: "Just a quick call here." "Just one little text." "I'll just be a minute." "This won't take me long." "Hang in there with me." "Almost done." "It'll be worse if I don't do it now."

Technology moves the benchmarks of time and, by extension, creates different conditions for patience, endurance, and perseverance. Technology increases the expectation of instant gratification while it lowers the bar for delayed satisfaction. Before, I was willing and even happy to wait five long minutes for my computer to boot up. Delayed gratification was within that five-minute mark. If it took that long now, though, I'd likely be on the phone to three different people demanding an immediate fix before even two minutes were up. Previously my anxiety level was never triggered because I expected to wait five minutes. Now my anxiety level would definitely be set off because I'd believe something was seriously wrong.

Having this kind of instantaneous expectation about technology is one thing. We've become almost immune to the miraculous. It's another thing, however, when we take that truncated panic-point and transfer it from technology onto people. After all, if I expect instant gratification from so many things in my life, if I expect other forces to come in and immediately relieve my internal tension, why not begin to view people and relationships the same way? Why can't people be as fast, responsive, and controllable as technology?

I become used to technology never telling me "no." People, however, tell me no all the time. When I'm driving and want to go faster without changing lanes, the driver up ahead tells me no. When I want a certain project at work done in a specific time frame, the person responsible tells me no by not getting it done within my expectations. I expect my wife to agree with my priorities for our evening and arrive home to find, no, she's decided on something else. I expect my preteen to act more like an adult in this situation when, no, he resolves to act decidedly his age. I expect my car repair to take three or four hours and find out, no, my car is going to be in the shop for two days.

Important things can be like glaciers; they are inexorable, ever moving but at a slower pace. Important things can build up immense momentum, but they do so over time.

People and life in general have a way of telling me no or, at least, not living up to my expectations. I plan a camping trip with the boys, and it rains all weekend. I'm late to an appointment and take a favorite shortcut, only to find a road crew has it down to one lane. I run to the store to get that certain brand, only to find it's sold out and they won't have any stocked until the next day. With each little no I can get more frustrated. With each little no my patience is stretched thinner and thinner. With each little no I find I have to wait and endure further discomfort and tension. Each little no often results in things taking more time than I expect them to. Tasks, duties, and obligations are left unresolved, to be dealt with another day. Life and people can, sometimes, seem like a continual series of no. And my threshold for when people begin to look more like problems and relationships more like roadblocks sinks lower and lower. The lower that threshold sinks, the less pleasant I am to be around; the more anxious and uncomfortable I feel, the more tempting it is to divert myself with technology.

As much as I complain, though, I do understand the priorities. Though I love my computer, I wouldn't trade a single relationship for it. That goes for my cell phone too. If I was given an ultimatum, I know where I'd stand.

I'm a little bit shakier, however, when it comes to everyday decisions with the technology surrounding my life. I have to constantly monitor how many times I let the urgent override the important. I have to remind myself that people are not programmable things and won't act as such. I have to remind myself to be patient, to take a deep breath, to turn off the panic button and relax, even if the network is down at work and I can't get any of my e-mails. I have to remind myself I am not always in control, nor should I be. That's just the way life is.

Sometimes I have to remind myself that *slow* is not a dirty word.

CONNECTION SECTION

The tighter you tie yourself to technology, the more warped your sense of time can become as your expectations of what is and what is not acceptable change. It can be difficult to extricate yourself from your current time frame in order to rediscover context for your feelings of unease, frustration, irritation, and anger when things don't happen as quickly as you think they should.

Sometimes I have to remind myself that *slow* is not a dirty word.

In order to help you quantify what your internal time frames are, I'd like you to answer the following questions:

1. When you call or text a person, how long do you expect it to take for that person to respond?

2. Are there people you avoid calling or texting because you know they are "slow" responders?

3. Who are your slow responders? Are they family or are they friends?

4. Do you text more than you call?

5. Do the people you communicate with respond better to texts than calls?

6. Do you respond more quickly to texts than calls? Why do you think that is?

7. When you're at the computer and something isn't working right, how long does it take before you get anxious or irritated?

8. Does technology, in general, make you anxious?

9. Do you understand how each of your devices work, or is it all sort of a mystery to you?

I've found when people understand the way things work—from how long it takes people to respond, to how the technology in that pocket-sized computer operates—they are more patient because their expectations more closely match reality. Understanding yourself and your unrecognized expectations can help you move your demands into a more realistic time frame. Then people and life will match your expectations, and you'll be less stressed, anxious, and resentful.

Now I'd like you to think about what your technology use was like ten years ago. What devices did you have? How long did they take? What amount of time did you consider "slow," and what amount of time did you consider "fast"?

Do that exercise again, but make the time range five years ago instead of ten.

Do that exercise again, but make the time range one year ago instead of five.

In what ways can you see your expectations changing over the past ten years? How is technology affecting your ability to wait, to have patience, to persevere through delayed gratification?

Are you a calmer person today than you were ten years ago? Are you better able to weather the storm of waiting? How has technology made waiting easier for you? How has it made it more difficult?

Understanding yourself and your unrecognized expectations can help you move your demands into a more realistic time frame.

The challenge is to use technology to enhance your life, including your ability to be patient and to wait. When I traveled, I used to get highly annoyed if a flight was delayed. Now, because of technology, my choices for using that time have significantly expanded. It makes it easier for me to relax and wait until whatever problem is fixed so I can get on my way. Also because of technology, I can easily and quickly let the people affected by the delayed flight know about my change in plans.

If I use technology to help me weather the wait, I'm fine. I just need to remember that technology can help me use time, not control it.

Chapter 8

THE ANGST OF OFF-LINE

MARIAN COULDN'T WAIT to get to the beach for a week of sheer bliss. She chattered on while happily packing the car. Cal didn't say much; it was hard to be excited. Already he was planning how he was going to pull off staying connected, despite his promise to Marian that he was actually going to "get away" this time.

The thought of relying on some backwater town paper or some random channel on local television was repugnant.

When he'd said that, he hadn't honestly meant it. Cal figured he'd be able to sneak in some laptop and phone use during times Marian wasn't around. He'd tell her he was going to stay inside and read a book while she went strolling down the beach, but he secretly planned to use her absence to go online. He figured as long as she didn't know, she'd be fine and he'd still be able to stay connected to work and, well, life. The thought of relying on some backwater town paper or some random channel on local television was repugnant. He needed to be connected.

If not for that huge nonrefundable deposit, he would have called off the whole thing upon discovering the beach house had no Internet connection. But Marian would not relent, insisting it was a way to "encourage" him to keep his promise. At least he had his cell phone ace-in-the-hole—until she'd reluctantly revealed the beach house was in a dead zone. But, she reminded him in terse, clipped tones, that shouldn't make a difference because the week was supposed to be about rest, relaxation, and their relationship. Now he was stuck ferreting out the nearest Wi-Fi hotspot in a town that boasted more seagulls than people.

It was a complication but one Cal was determined to work around. Bringing his laptop would be too much of a giveaway, but he clearly needed his phone for safety on the drive to the beach, so she couldn't argue about that. He could do without the laptop if he at least had his phone.

Disconnecting for an entire week was just not an option, no matter what he said to Marian. He knew himself and knew he'd go absolutely out of his mind. It wasn't just the sheer boredom that bothered him; rather, it was being out of the loop. Cal needed to be *in* the loop, *working* the loop, *directing* the loop. Who knew what kind of chaos could erupt over seven long, disconnected days? Cal was determined not to find out.

Coffee; that's the tactic he'd use. He just needed to find a coffee shop. Coffee shops were never isolated; they always nestled with other busy shops, which meant some kind of "downtown" core. Business hubs had to have cell coverage, and coffee shops were known for sporting Wi-Fi access. He'd tell her it was his "alone time" in the morning. He'd even offer to bring back her favorite drink. Marian could surely grant him thirty minutes every morning for his "alone time," as long as the other twenty-three and a half hours were hers—unplugged.

Cal stopped and took a deep breath; it was going to be a very long week.

DISCONNECT ANGST

The word *angst* means a feeling of anxiety, apprehension, or insecurity. I think the best-known use of the word comes from the phrase *teenage angst*, which describes the rocky, turbulent, emotional roller coaster of adolescence. But *teenage angst* may have found a close competitor in *disconnect angst*—the feeling of anxiety, apprehension, or insecurity when forced to live life off-line.

Not long ago a Canadian firm, Solutions Research Group, conducted a study entitled, "Age of Disconnect Anxiety and Four Reasons Why It's Difficult to Stay

"If Thine Eye Offend Thee..."

If you think it's hard to disconnect now, when all it takes is to simply put down that gadget and walk away, it'll only get harder as computing technology becomes part of our wardrobe, our accessories, and even our bodies.

In 2011 a group of researchers at the University of Washington successfully tested a contact lens that could not only improve functional eyesight but also included integrated wireless displays. Think: a computer monitor...*in your eye.* These contact lenses are a significant step along the way to developing unobtrusive "wearable computers" that keep one visually, tactilely, and wirelessly in contact with "the grid" at all hours of the day.[1]

At that point, going "offline" may require nothing short of a miracle.

Off the Grid."[2] News stories and blog posts using the term "disconnect anxiety" immediately followed, generally agreeing with the cyber-equivalent of nodding heads. For most, the very thought of living off-line produced sympathetic (if not actual) anxiety. The term resonated.

The study described disconnect anxiety as "various feelings of disorientation and nervousness experienced when a person is deprived of Internet or wireless access for a period of time." Nearly seven out of ten people surveyed reported experiencing some level of anxiety when disconnected (27 percent reported elevated symptoms, while 41 percent reported only occasional anxiety). The rest, 32 percent, reported little or no anxiety being off-line.

The very thought of living off-line produced sympathetic (if not actual) anxiety.

The demographics of the 27 percent who reported elevated anxiety symptoms were interesting:

- Forty-one percent were ages twelve to twenty-four.
- Fifty percent were twenty-five to forty-nine.
- Nine percent were over the age of fifty.

At first I was mildly distressed that the beginning age of reporting was twelve—until I remembered my own kids and the age they got their first cell phones. Upon reflection, I then wondered why the youngest generation didn't come in with even higher numbers than the middle range. This was until I thought about how people my age and younger are wedded to our technology—for work, for play, for family, for everything. I could completely understand the lowest number represented those over fifty, as this is the generation of people who have personal experience that life is possible without gadgetry.

Interestingly, I found a teenager's high school paper disputing the relevance of "disconnect anxiety" to teenagers.[3] The author posited that the real by-product of teenage cell phone deprivation was understimulation or boredom, not anxiety. While I understand why a teenager would consider *under*stimulation stressful, the test subjects she used knew beforehand that they were going to be without their cell phones and agreed to the withdrawal (weeding out those whose reaction was "No way!"). Additionally, these teens knew their time of deprivation would be relatively short.

In no way do I intend to disparage the excellent work done by this teenager, Michelle Hackman (who won second place in the 2011 Intel Science Talent Search[4] for her work, which is impressive). Incidentally, the idea for the paper came to her when she noticed a group of her peers all sitting around together, texting. She wondered what would happen if they were separated from their cell phones and would that reaction be akin to an addictive withdrawal.

Teenagers may get bored after going forty-five minutes without their cell phones to provide stimulation, but that boredom would shift to genuine anxiety if the amount of disconnected time was significantly longer. A recent study by McCann Workgroup showed just how much teenagers value their online connectivity: more than half of seven thousand survey participants from different countries, ages sixteen to thirty, said they would rather give up their sense of smell in order to stay connected.[5]

Think about that for a minute. The researchers didn't ask about hearing or sight—you need those senses to interpret an online world.

Instead, they chose the sense of smell to jettison, something vital and necessary for real life but superfluous in the virtual realm (at least until scratch-and-sniff goes digital). Granted, this was a hypothetical scenario, but it shows how integral staying connected has become: young people would rather sacrifice an essential part of their humanity on the altar of technology than give up technology itself.

Teenagers may get bored after going forty-five minutes without their cell phones to provide stimulation, but that boredom would shift to genuine anxiety if the amount of disconnected time was significantly longer.

This need to stay connected appears to be universal or, at least, global. In 2010 the International Center for Media and the Public Agenda (ICMPA) partnered with the Salzburg Academy on Media and Global Change to conduct a worldwide study called "Unplugged."[6] They asked one thousand students from ten countries across five continents to abstain from using media (television, radio, the Internet, and cell phones) for twenty-four hours.

Apparently, this online angst is not a uniquely American phenomenon. From ICMPA's website, here are the ten universities where students were selected:

- American University of Beirut (Lebanon)

- Bournemouth University, Dorset (United Kingdom)

- Chinese University of Hong Kong (China/Hong Kong)

- Chongqing University, Chongqing (China/mainland)

- Hofstra University (New York)

- Hong Kong Shue Yan University (China/Hong Kong)

- Makerere University, Kampala (Uganda)

- Pontificia Universidad Católica Argentina, Buenos Aires (Argentina)

- Pontificia Universidad Catolica de Chile, Santiago (Chile)

- Universidad Iberoamericana, Mexico City (Mexico)

- University of St. Cyril and Methodius, Trnava (Slovakia)

That's quite a list! But so is the list of experiences shared by the participants:

- Students described their tether to technology as an addiction, including feelings of withdrawal.

- A majority found they couldn't go completely without media either because of personal failure or because it was simply everywhere around them and they couldn't avoid it even if they'd agreed to.

- Students reported a loss of self with the loss of their cell phones, as these devices contain their virtual identities.

- Technology is the way students connect and organize their social lives, with the most common gateway being Facebook.

- Students select different media venues for different categories of people they interact with. For example, they call a parent but text a friend. They hop on Facebook to see what the larger group is doing. For interacting with adults, in school or work, they e-mail. It's like dressing in a work uniform or sweats depending upon what you're doing or who you're with. Students use these various media to define how others view them and how they view themselves.

- Students realized not only are their relationships interwoven with media, but, for some, their dominant relationship was with media itself. Loss of media for those twenty-four hours left them confronting significant feelings of loneliness.

- This seventh point touched upon Michelle Hackman's theory about teen boredom. The ICMPA study found students didn't know what to do with themselves when they couldn't turn to media. Not only were they bored without media, but also they were bored quickly as media-hyped attention spans went into numbing slow-motion.

- Cell phones offered connection, comfort, and security—"this generation's Swiss Army knife and its security blanket"—a feeling that crossed national and ethnic lines.

- For the plugged generation, *news* describes a friend's status update as much as it describes a global weather event. News meant any piece of new information, no matter the source or the subject. Students chose where to gather this news, eschewing traditional media outlets for social media like Twitter or Facebook.

- Students don't have to look for news; they "inhale" it from the ubiquitous media atmosphere. Media find them 24/7.

Students realized not only are their relationships interwoven with media, but, for some, their dominant relationship was with media itself.

- Less is more. Students reported that 140 characters is all that's needed to convey the news unless it's something they're personally interested in. They have neither the time nor the interest to delve any further.

- Television is a zone-out, activity done with friends to relax and, presumably, take a break from other media.

- Music is a mood-regulator and makes boring activities like commuting tolerable.

- E-mail equals older. Students use it for work and to communicate with professors. It's more formal, like having to dress in a suit; they'll do it for a short list of reasons.

- Abstaining from media helped them understand just how hooked they are and allowed them to revert to

"simple pleasures" like actually talking to people in
the same room without texting or listening to music
at the same time.

I can't say I was surprised. Irritatingly, much of this resonates with me. What struck me, though, was the consensus among these students about their media use and their giddy relief that the experiment (which many would not do again) was only for a single day. Again, these are people who *agreed* to the experiment to go twenty-four hours without media. I can only imagine what the reactions would have been if people had been forced to go without media for, say, a full week.

Did these students learn a great deal from their digital deprivation? I believe they did. So did I, because I contend this urge to stay connected is not just experienced by teenagers and young adults; it affects us all.

Technological Tethers

The Solutions Research Group report, replicating much of what was identified by students in the ICMPA study, identified four ways people experience disconnect anxiety:

1. *Safety:* People can feel anxiety where a cell phone is perceived as a "lifeline" or a "safety net."

2. *Work:* People can feel anxious when out of "the flow" (both the flow of work and general information), which must be monitored in order to stay current, valued, and competitive.

3. *Social:* People can feel anxious, fearful of missing out on social events or missing access to insider tidbits of information that constitute the new "social currency."

4. *Navigation:* People can feel anxious being without the device that tells you where you should be and what you should be doing and that holds all your personal data.

This urge to stay connected is not just experienced by teenagers and young adults; it affects us all.

As we connect ourselves with more technological tethers, we increasingly anchor them to our sense of safety, self-worth, social connection, and security. It used to be the word *disconnect* had two common meanings: you were disconnected from a phone call, or you disconnected from reality. Who would have thought those two definitions would merge? Now, being disconnected from your phone *is* being disconnected from reality—at least, we've allowed it to feel that way.

Here are a few of the words and phrases used to describe what being disconnected feels like, according to the study: *feeling lost, half a voice, disoriented, panic, tense, empty, inadequate, dazed, getting behind info flow, loss of freedom.* One of those terms stood out to me: *disoriented.*

Why would being disconnected from a physical device make you feel disoriented? Disorientation is caused when you lose your bearings, when you are displaced from your normal position or relationship. Thus, if your sense of self is tethered to one of these devices, disconnecting *will* be disorienting. If your normal position in daily life is to rely on these devices for safety, work, social, and navigation purposes, even the thought of being without is going to produce anxiety. If you have placed a priority on the relationship you have with technology, being without that primary relationship, even for a little while, will make you feel deprived.

Disorientation can also mean losing your sense of time, place, or identity. It's almost as if we've invested a significant portion of ourselves inside these devices. When we're separated from our gadgets, we become disoriented and lose the sense of where and who we are. It is no wonder, then, we become anxious, apprehensive, and insecure when forced to disconnect.

In chapter 2, "Multi-Taxed," we talked about how using these devices can increase our sense of anxiety and stress. In this chapter we've talked about how not using these devices can produce the same thing. This idea was echoed in the study. One participant wrote, "Computers and technology may make our lives easier from some aspects, but they have also caused us to place urgency on everything, and I always feel rushed."[7]

When we're separated from our gadgets, we become disoriented and lose the sense of where and who we are.

So, *with* technology we feel anxious, and *without* technology we feel anxious. We need to stop placing ourselves in no-win situations.

The way to get over this disconnect anxiety is to figure out why we feel it in the first place. While the devices we use may exacerbate and magnify anxiety, they don't create it: we do. We need to understand how these devices trigger that anxiety so we can avoid it. (For more on anxiety and stress, I encourage you to get information about my book *Overcoming Anxiety, Worry and Fear: Practical Ways to Find Peace* at www.aplaceofhope.com.)

SAFETY

One of the primary reasons I gave my kids a cell phone was for their safety. I wanted them to be able to contact me whenever they needed. But, honestly, I also wanted to be able to get a hold of them. My kids are fairly young and are generally with me or my wife most of the time—but not all of the time. Hence the cell phone. Parents of older teens tell me that feeling of needing to keep your kids safe where your kids are concerned only gets stronger over time. As my kids increasingly venture out in the world on their own, I want to know we all have direct and instant access to each other. So, yes, having a cell phone is a safety issue.

If I have a flat tire or an accident, I want to be able to call for help. I feel safer knowing my cell phone is handy. But if I didn't bring my cell phone or if I didn't have coverage, should I necessarily feel anxious? Does having my cell phone provide any actual protection against a flat tire or an accident? Of course not. In my mind I've created hypothetical scenarios where possessing a cell phone means safety; therefore, lacking a cell phone means danger. But is not having a cell phone truly unsafe, in and of itself? Again, the answer is no. My safety is dependent upon a variety of factors, only one of which is whether or not I have access to my cell phone.

Anxiety, however, is a fear response that ignores nuance: it can escalate to full-fledged panic quickly with little or no evidence. Once I've decided having a cell phone means safety, anxiety quickly concludes that not having a cell phone is dangerous and unsafe. *But that isn't true.* Generally, with or without a cell phone, I am not in unsafe situations.

> ### Technology:
> ### The Show of Wisdom Without the Reality
>
> An overreliance on technology is not a new phenomenon or risk. In 360 B.C. Plato recorded an account of a conversation between two mythological gods, Thamus and Theuth. When Theuth proudly shows off his invention, writing and the use of letters, Thamus replies with a warning:
>
> "O most ingenious Theuth, the parent or inventor of an art is not always the best judge of the utility or inutility of his own inventions to the users of them. And in this instance, you who are the father of letters, from a paternal love of your own children have been led to attribute to them a quality which they cannot have; for this discovery of yours will create forgetfulness in the learners' souls, because they will not use their memories; they will trust to the external written characters and not remember of themselves. The specific which you have discovered is an aid not to memory, but to reminiscence, and you give your disciples not truth, but only the semblance of truth; they will be hearers of many things and will have learned nothing; they will appear to be omniscient and will generally know nothing; they will be tiresome company, having the show of wisdom without the reality."[8]

The primary factor in my sense of safety cannot be my cell phone. If it is, though I'm in no danger, I will feel unnecessarily unsafe without my cell phone. Conversely, I might feel unnecessarily safe when I do have my cell phone despite actual risk. Safety is determined by a combination of conditions and circumstances having little to do with cell phones. It is not my cell phone that makes me safe but my own ability to analyze and evaluate those conditions and circumstances and make safe choices.

WORK

Do you remember back in chapter 2, we discussed sufficers and maximizers, and type A and type B people? One of the almost comical statistics from this Solutions Research Group study that made the rounds on the blogs was that three out of five of Blackberry users admitted to taking their device in the bathroom (63 percent), along with two out of five laptop users (37 percent). Three out of five people (63 percent) also agreed with the statement, "I'm the kind of person who likes to be in touch all the time."[9] Apparently they weren't kidding when they said "all the time." I venture to guess that maximizer, type A personalities experience greater levels of disconnect anxiety than sufficer, type B personalities and are probably more apt to require their electronic devices in the bathroom.

If the boss is e-mailing you at ten-thirty on a Saturday night, are you supposed to respond? What happens if you do? What happens if you don't? What happens if that obnoxious coworker who sits next to you responds before you do?

I wonder how people would have responded if the researchers had changed the statement from, "I'm the kind of person who *likes* to be in touch all the time," to "I'm the kind of person who *needs* to be in touch all the time." After all, if you are compelled to take your device with you even into the bathroom, I suggest "like" is closer to "need."

It is no accident that these statistics were in the portion of the study dealing with work. There is such a frenetic drive to produce, to keep current, to stay on top, to avoid slipping in the employment environment. Competition is real in the workplace, and many feel anxiety over their employment situation. If the boss is e-mailing you at ten-thirty on a Saturday night, are you supposed to respond? What happens if you do? What happens if you don't? What happens if that obnoxious coworker who sits next to you responds before you do? Does that mean she'll gain status and favor over you? All of this produces anxiety because work is money and money is security.

As the boundaries between home and work and access blur, you may decide that if you *can* be online, you *should* be online, whether it's during typical work hours or not. So you feel compelled to be online, constantly checking "the flow." Not knowing what is happening and what you're missing is stressful and makes you anxious, so you relieve that anxiety through constant monitoring.

It's said, "No vacation goes unpunished." It plays on the cliché "No good deed goes unpunished" and is just recognition that in today's world, with the flood of information we have to deal with, being disconnected from work for very long carries its own punishment. There's all the extra work to prepare for a vacation, then all the extra work to recover from one. I'm sure there are some jobs where you can just leave and have all of your tasks, duties, and obligations handled by someone else in your absence, but those are the exception, not the rule.

Sometimes it can seem so troublesome to take a vacation that it hardly seems worth it. I read a story recently about the amount of unused vacation time American workers leave on the table every year. Last year the figure was $67 billion—that's billion with a *b*.[10] We're not using all of our vacation, and more and more of us, even while on vacation, are making sure to go online to work at least once a day to clear out e-mail and just keep track of what's going on.

SOCIAL

There used to be these quaint square paper things that would come in the mail. They were called "invitations" to real-world events, and they provided details such as what, when, where, and who. You could stick them on your fridge as a reminder so you wouldn't forget. They came days, weeks, sometimes months, before the event. The more important the event, the more advance notice you got. They were very handy, but they have now become somewhat obsolete for everything but wedding and graduation announcements.

Then there were the invitations that came over the phone. Someone actually called to invite you to, and sometimes even to remind you about, the event. If they didn't talk to you in person, they left a message with all the information you needed to be sure to attend.

You don't have to mail, phone, or e-mail invitations. All you need to do is announce your event on your wall. How easy is that?

Then invitations switched to e-mail. You could send a single invitation to a variety of people. Now invitees had all the information in written form, without having to write it down themselves. They could reply to your e-mail and let you know if they were coming or not. This didn't always happen, and the incidence of reply seemed to correlate with the age of the recipient: the older the person, the more likely you were to get a reply, but not always.

Now, there's Facebook. You don't have to mail, phone, or e-mail invitations. All you need to do is announce your event on your wall. How easy is that? You don't have to put yourself out for anybody; they have to come to you to get the information. It shows who your real, committed friends are, right?

Welcome to the social angst inherent in this brave new world. As the television show *The X Files* used to say, "The truth is out there," and you better find it so you're not left out. People are not necessarily going to push the information to you; you need to be online so you can pull the information to yourself. And it's not just parties or events that you need to pull; you also need to pull tidbits, factoids, and even gossip, rumors, and the latest buzz.

Once you have the buzz, now it is incumbent upon you to pass it along, so you need to be connected with other friends you can tag, text, or call. If you're disconnected, how will you know who is trying to get hold of you and why? There's a stream of consciousness to your social circle, and you'd better have access.

Silence used to be called golden, but now it's apocalyptic. "What am I missing?" used to be a casual question; now it's an imperative, fraught with anxiety.

It's not enough, now, to simply know something. The primary factor in your social cachet is how *quickly* you know it and how many people learn about it from you and not some other source.

I've been intrigued by a mobile phone commercial that is highly instructive regarding the social anxiety component of technology. In it, four people are riding in a car, all of them accessing their cell phones. A man in the backseat downloads his message more quickly than the others and begins to laugh aloud, exclaiming, "That's so funny!" A few seconds later the rest of the occupants of the car (except the driver) "get" the joke on their phones and also begin to laugh. Finally, the woman in the backseat turns to the first man laughingly, who dismisses her, already bored and ready to move on.[11] The message is clear: you don't want to be left behind, not even for a few seconds. What kind of pressure does that put on people?

NAVIGATION

Of all the anxiety-producing categories, this is the one I identify with most. I have practically transferred my brain into my cell phone: it has archived all the names, places, dates, numbers, reminders, and notations—everything I can't be troubled to remember. The first thing I do every morning is to check my calendar app to see what's waiting for me. Without my cell phone, I would truly feel lost. The amount of time and energy it would take to restore all that data is immense. The only time I'm ever really tempted to kiss a stranger is when the clerk at the phone store transfers my old SIM card into my new phone.

The message is clear: you don't want to be left behind, not even for a few seconds. What kind of pressure does that put on people?

Cell phones permit me to not remember things, one of their most redeeming qualities. I worry I'll forget to do that one vitally important thing mixed in with all the other urgent things in my day. My cell phone, my surrogate brain, is more reliable than I am. I joke that my goal in life is not to have to remember anything but my cell phone. It's said ironically, with my tongue planted firmly in cheek, but it's truer than I want it to be.

Because of the amount of pictures and data that can be stored on our cell phones and accessed through our computers, we transfer ourselves over into this technology. The more importance and necessity we invest into this transfer, the more tied to it we are. And then, for some unknown reason, we can't access ourselves. We feel empty, adrift, left on our own to navigate the day, and we just feel lost. We're terrified we're going to forget something important, miss something vital, or lose out on an opportunity.

In this kind of pressure-cooker world, there is no room for error. The technology is there to perfectly manage our lives, from the time we wake up with our cell phone's alarm to the time we use an app to shut the lights out and dock the phone for some soothing night music, and everything in between. Each minute of every hour is regulated and controlled so we get where we're supposed to go and don't make any mistakes, like missing a meeting or a school play (unless we have another meeting and then, that's work, and it's just for this one night). Being disconnected means relying solely on yourself to navigate your day, and you know how that's gone in the past. Better not to chance it—so you have to be online. If you're not, there's no telling whom you'll let down. The only thing you're sure of is the first one to fall is going to be you.

CONNECTION SECTION

It's time to place yourself in an uncomfortable position. I want you to envision what it's like when you're off-line. If you're truly brave, you can actually go off-line and document how long it takes you to start figuratively climbing the walls. How long does it take for that skin-crawling sensation to start? One hour? Six hours? Twelve hours? A day? Two days? Three? At what point does the panic set in

The Angst of Off-Line

and your inner, deprived self starts screaming it's been too long and you just have to go back online?

Think about what your panicked voice is saying to you. What dire possibility is being presented to you as an increasing certainty?

What activity causes you the most anxiety? Not using your cell phone? Not texting? No Facebook? No Twitter? No e-mail?

For each activity you normally engage in, what is the most uncomfortable thing about being off-line?

Are you more worried that you aren't able to make contact with others or that others are not able to make contact with you?

What do you imagine people will think if they don't hear from you?

In the survey described in this chapter, several words and phrases were given by other people to describe how they felt when disconnected. They were:

- Feeling lost

- Half a voice

- Disoriented

- Panic

- Tense

- Empty

- Dazed

- Inadequate

- Getting behind info flow

- Loss of freedom

Which ones do you identify with? Is it a feeling you associate with being off-line in general or not having access to a particular device?

If you had to give up only one of your devices for a week (cell phone, computer, game console, notebook, iPad, Kindle, etc.), which one would you give up first? Which one would you give up last?

Angst was described in this chapter as a feeling of anxiety, apprehension, and insecurity. How does being off-line trigger each of these feelings in you?

There were also four areas of anxiety identified by the study referenced. Evaluate each area, given your own technology uses and patterns, and choose whether you feel "elevated" anxiety, "occasional" anxiety, or "little/no" anxiety. Why is that?

- Safety

- Work

- Social

- Navigation

Would you voluntarily go a day disconnected? A week? A month? Why or why not?

You may come to recognize that your tether to technology has stretched itself tight, leaving you little room to disconnect without discomfort and feelings of withdrawal.

Think about the last time you went on vacation or spent extended time away with family or friends. How much time did you spend connecting over the Internet, texting, or phoning each day? Did anyone talk to you about your use or ask you to cut back so you could spend more time and be more present?

Has a family member or friend asked you to stop being online so you could be more present with him or her? If so, how did you react? How did you feel at that moment?

Michelle Hackman wanted to know if teens would exhibit withdrawal symptoms if they were kept from going online. Withdrawal happens when you develop a physical or psychological dependence to something and then stop. Withdrawal symptoms can include preoccupation with the stopped activity, irritability, trouble sleeping, poor concentration, and strong urges to continue the activity. You may come to recognize that your tether to technology has stretched itself tight, leaving you little room to disconnect without discomfort and feelings of withdrawal. If so, recognize and accept it. Keep your eyes, heart, and mind open as you go about your day, more alert to technology's hold over you.

And keep reading, even though you're really uncomfortable.

Chapter 9

TRANSFER OF POWER

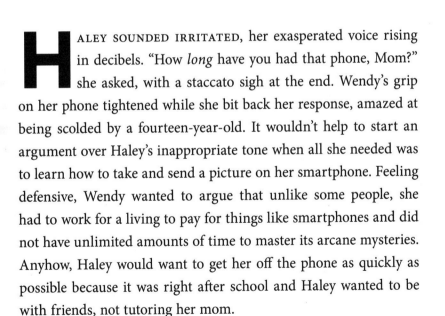

HALEY SOUNDED IRRITATED, her exasperated voice rising in decibels. "How *long* have you had that phone, Mom?" she asked, with a staccato sigh at the end. Wendy's grip on her phone tightened while she bit back her response, amazed at being scolded by a fourteen-year-old. It wouldn't help to start an argument over Haley's inappropriate tone when all she needed was to learn how to take and send a picture on her smartphone. Feeling defensive, Wendy wanted to argue that unlike some people, she had to work for a living to pay for things like smartphones and did not have unlimited amounts of time to master its arcane mysteries. Anyhow, Haley would want to get her off the phone as quickly as possible because it was right after school and Haley wanted to be with friends, not tutoring her mom.

"I know, I know," she said, mollifying her daughter. "Look, just walk me through it real quick," she asked again, making sure she had something to write with. Haley's instructions were short and fast and assumed she knew way more about the stupid phone than she did. It was humiliating enough to have to call about the picture, but she needed it for work and didn't have time to google the instruction manual, let alone try to decipher it. Predictably Haley gave rapid-fire instructions, in an aggrieved tone of voice, with an aside to her listening friends that she had to tell her mother how to work the camera app. Great, now the Gang of Four, as she lovingly referred to Haley's girlfriends, could be amused at her expense.

The two of them seemed constantly at odds and out of sync; this whole ridiculous phone episode was just one more reminder.

Wendy disliked these teenage years. She could *so* do without the attitude and the arguing, the disasters and the drama. Most of all, she disliked being made to feel *old*. Wendy was barely in her forties and resented the constant adolescent innuendo that she was somehow past her shelf life. She didn't understand or appreciate the current fashion trends but was still somehow expected to pay for them. Overnight, it seemed, Wendy had been moved from Haley's "us" category to "them" in order to make room for the Gang of Four. At the very time Wendy was looking forward to connecting to Haley, remembering her own teenage years and missing that camaraderie, she was shut out, left on stand-by in a rarely used corner of Haley's social sphere. The two of them seemed constantly at odds and out of sync; this whole ridiculous phone episode was just one more reminder. Irritated, Wendy promised herself that she would spend time going over that phone so she didn't have to ask Haley for anything about it again, all the while knowing she probably wouldn't do it and would continue to ask.

ROLE REVERSAL

If you're a parent of a teenager or an older middle-schooler, you probably remember that evening when your child brought home his or her math homework and asked you to help. Because school is a priority, you were happy to oblige—until confronted with the assignment in question. Nothing made any sense. This wasn't the way you remembered it. It's hard enough dredging those decades-old formulas from the recesses of your brain, but even after surfacing, they bore no relation to what was being asked. You were at a total loss; up to that point you'd been a magician, sagely pulling answers out of thin air to the awe and amazement of your child. Now you're being lectured on the fundamentals of algebra.

The disappointment is obvious; you're supposed to *know* this stuff and you don't. You don't have a clue what's going on or how to help. Both of you are amazingly short-tempered: you, because you're expected to know everything and don't; your child, because you're expected to know everything and don't. With this math assignment a wedge has been driven into your relationship and a marker placed. You are no longer as omnipotent and universally useful as you've been in the past. Your child has become aware that there's knowledge in this world he possesses that you do not. You have experienced a transfer of power.

What used to happen around early adolescence in math now happens on a regular basis with technology. Depending upon your age, it may have started with the VCR (the venerable videocassette recorder: VCRs were to movies what eight-track tapes were to music). These were amazing devices, you could connect them to your television and play VHS tapes right out of the box. Of course, to set it up correctly was enough to send most people over the edge of patience into snappy irritability. There were all those wires, with all those colors that had to go in just the right way or the thing didn't work, and it seemed like you had to try every possible color combination to find the right one—unless you asked your teenager who casually walked over and said, "Oh, you just need to do this," leaving you wavering between intense gratitude and volcanic frustration. Then, once you got the whole thing working on screen, you still had the issue of the blinking 12:00. Most people tended to wait days, weeks, months, and even years with that twelve just continuing to blink. Why? Because they didn't understand the technology well enough to set the clock to the right time. They used the VCR but they didn't master it, and they had neither the patience nor the desire to learn.

Since the VCR, technology has taken a quantum leap in number and complexity of devices. There aren't just internal little clocks to worry about; there are internal little computers. Parents may buy the technology, but, for many, their kids are the ones with the patience and desire to learn how to use it. The older the parent, the greater is the disparity between generational technology knowhow and comfort. Parents buy a gadget for one or two functions; teens figure out how to use it for twenty. Kids maneuver around this technology with the ease of an accomplished race car driver. It's almost second nature.

Kids don't use a manual to find out how to use the device; they use the device to find out how it works. They let the device teach them.

How is it that eight-year-old kids have an intuitive way of grasping the very technology their thirty-eight-year-old parent just purchased? It hardly seems fair. I think it is because kids approach technology from a different point of view than adults. Kids see technology as exciting and fun; they aren't more worried about breaking it than using it. They aren't concerned about cost because

---

Do as I Say, Not as I Lie Online

A recent article in the *Los Angeles Times* began with these two chilling lines: "Millions of kids under the age of 13 have signed up for Facebook. And their parents helped them lie to do it."

If a twelve-year old signed up for an account on Facebook, not only would it violate the site's Terms of Service, it would also violate the current Children's Online Privacy Protection Act (COPPA), a Federal law restricting websites from collecting information from children under the age of thirteen.

So, a senior researcher with Microsoft Research coordinated a survey with other researchers from Northwestern University, UC Berkeley, and Harvard in order to determine how prevalent underage users were on social media sites like Facebook.

The survey revealed that more than half of all parents with kids under thirteen knew their kids were using Facebook. (Among parents with ten-year-olds, one in five knew their kids were using the site.)

Nearly seven in ten parents helped their kids set up their profiles.

Nearly seven in ten parents helped their kids lie.[1]

167

they didn't buy it. They have time to sit down with it and say, "I wonder what this does?" They don't use a manual to find out how to use the device; they use the device to find out how it works. They let the device teach them, in whatever roundabout way their exploration takes them. It's exploring; it's fun.

Further, if their friends have the same or similar device, they compare notes and learn from each other. They can tech-talk, and many of the adults around them won't understand the language. It's like having a secret club or a secret code. They experience a transfer of power.

ALL ACCESS

When I grew up, parents held the keys to access, literally. Before I was street legal, if I wanted to see my friends, a parent had to drive me. Of course, there were all sorts of conditions for when I saw my friends, which ones, for how long, only on certain days, and at certain times. My access to my friends was limited, and I could only have it when I'd fulfilled duties like homework and household chores. We had "family time" on Sundays, which was a friends blackout (only family at the house on Sunday). I couldn't even talk on the phone for long because there was only one line (this is one of my "walk a mile in the snow" stories).

With technology, parents no longer have such tight control over access. Your teenager may not be able to physically leave the house, but he or she can be connected to friends on the phone, by texting, on Facebook, and over the Internet. Access is no longer easily limited or controlled by parents. There has been a transfer of power.

It's the same with other media. Previously parents controlled the television (and there were a limited number of channels). Now the choices are legion, and teens are utilizing more and more of it.

What they can't watch on the television itself they can access online using their cell phones, iPods, or notebooks. Unless a parent wants to become surgically attached to their teenager, it's very difficult to know, let alone control, what and whom their kids have access to. They have the power to connect in a multitude of ways, all provided usually (thank you very much) by the very parents who now marvel at the implications.

Teens spend as much time with their media as parents do at work. When you add in school and sleep, it's amazing how little time is left.

According to a Kaiser Family Foundation study, kids age eight through eighteen spend almost seven and a half hours awash in media every day. Factoring in their ability to multitask (listening to music while browsing Facebook, for example), their media exposure rises to ten hours and forty-five minutes per day, every day.[2] That's a huge amount of time watching television, surfing the Web, talking on the cell phone, texting, watching DVDs, and listening to music. Teens spend as much time with their media as parents do at work. When you add in school and sleep, it's amazing how little time is left.

LEAD BY FOLLOWING

While you might think teens are leading the technology charge instead of you, it's actually the opposite. The Barna Group published a study titled *The Family and Technology Report: How Technology Is Helping Families—and Where They Need Help.* In it they came to a very interesting conclusion: parents are modeling this huge consumption of media to their kids. You are transferring your use of all of these gadgets and devices over to them. According to the Barna study, "In fact, it is not kids who have brought the widespread use of technology into the home, it is us." The report goes on to note that parents in the study reported they used their cell phones even more regularly than their kids, were more apt to use a desktop computer, and equally apt to use a laptop or notebook.[3]

So, we are the ones who bring all these devices and technology into the lives of our families—and then decry the resulting lack of relationship. It's no wonder our kids consider us hypocrites. We tell them to get off Facebook but spend hours at night handling e-mail. We set rules about texting at the dinner table but leave the television on during the same meal. We track and limit the time they're on the computer, but we leave the television on even when no one is watching it. When our actions fail to live up to our words, we model a hypocritical double standard. Then, when confronted with our double standard, we abandon the defense of our reasoning and capitulate to our kids. When we capitulate, we transfer power.

We buy all of these things, for ourselves and for our kids, and then rely on our kids to teach us how to use them. Our kids are teaching us but not necessarily in ways we imagined. For example, consider the cell phones most teenagers have—according to a study by the Pew Research Center, 72 percent of them do.[4] Here are a couple more of the summary points from that Pew study about teens and cell phones:

When our actions fail to live up to our words, we model a hypocritical double standard. Then, when confronted with our double standard, we abandon the defense of our reasoning and capitulate to our kids.

- Teens are more apt to text their friends than call them.

- Of the vast majority of teens who text, more than half send fifty-plus messages per day. One-third send more than one hundred messages per day, and nearly one out of six (15 percent) send more than two hundred messages per day.

- Girls and boys text differently: girls send and receive an average of eighty messages per day, while for boys it's an average of thirty messages per day.

- Teens do more with their phones than just text or talk. They also take pictures (83 percent) and share those pictures (64 percent), play music (60 percent), and play games (46 percent). They go online (27 percent) and access social networks (23 percent).

Of those kids with a cell phone, almost nine out of ten use it for texting (88 percent). Texting has become the preferred way to communicate by teenagers, not e-mail.[5] I live in e-mail; most people my age do. Not so for younger people: texting is the new e-mail. Teens say they like texting because it's easier and more convenient than talking. In other words, they are in charge of whether they text, what they text, and when they text. Interestingly, teens say they will avoid answering their cell phones in order to train people to text them instead of calling them. This has forced parents to take up texting, even when they don't like it, because it's the only way to get their teens to answer. Training their parents is a way to transfer power.

Teens in charge of their phones and what they do with it and how they use it can have negative consequences. The Pew study found the 15 percent of teens say they've gotten a sexually suggestive, nude, or nearly nude picture of someone they know by text. *Of someone they know.* Of course, parents would be mortified if their teenager received such a picture, but imagine how you'd react as a parent if your teenager was the sender.

I read in my paper about a local man facing charges of distributing child pornography. He's twenty years old, and he hacked into the e-mail of an eighteen-year-old young woman, gaining access to and manipulating her information, pictures, and passwords. In doing so, he allegedly ran across topless pictures she'd taken of herself for her boyfriend when she was fifteen or sixteen but just never deleted. Now he is charged with distributing child pornography after forwarding those pictures to everyone in her e-mail address book, including friends, classmates, relatives, and potential employers. According to the story, "They ended up going out to her grandparents and teachers who she had asked for letters of recommendation."[6] E-mail, apparently, wasn't enough as her Facebook account was also hacked into and the pictures posted.

This same man is also alleged to have hacked into the e-mail account of a second young woman, also eighteen. There he found topless photos of her as well, which he posted to her MySpace page, then changed her password and settings, allowing anyone and everyone to access her photos. One of the young women said she knew the man and that he'd admitted hacking into her account. The other young woman had never met him but said they were friends on Facebook. According to the police, Facebook gave him access to personal data that "could have aided him in hacking into her accounts."[7]

When I read stories like this, I tend to run headlong into that brick wall of denial: I want to say "not my kid, not my family!" I don't want to believe that the cell phone I've given my oldest could be used as a conduit for pornography. I don't want to believe that time spent on that game system I've given my youngest could become more important than time spent with me. I don't want to believe that by giving my kids a fast and easy way to find answers online, I'm shortchanging their ability for contemplation, to dig deep to find hard-to-discover answers. I don't want to believe that my failure, lack of interest, or techno-savvy could cause me to overlook a potential danger to my kids through the very thing I wrapped up and gave as a Christmas or birthday gift.

This technology is powerful. I know this is true in my own life; how can I overlook it in my kids' lives? As a parent I need to be aware of the influence I have on my kids through my use of technology. What am I saying to them about what I consider important, valuable, worth my time and effort? When I give my kids technology to use for one purpose, it may be used for something completely different, something I can't approve of.

I don't want to believe that my failure, lack of interest, or techno-savvy could cause me to overlook a potential danger to my kids through the very thing I wrapped up and gave as a Christmas or birthday gift.

I often feel like nothing more than a glorified unpaid taxi service for all the events and activities my kids enjoy. Sometimes I wistfully think about what it will be like when they can drive themselves. I wouldn't even consider, though, giving my preteen the keys to my car and telling him to go have fun driving around the neighborhood at his age because of the danger involved. I understand the threat driving poses to kids until they're ready and have learned the fundamentals. I have to stop and wonder, though, if I've placed my kids prematurely into the "driver's seat" of some of this technology without the same consideration for their age and readiness to handle the consequences. Maybe, as a parent, I need to hold on to that power just a little while longer.

When kids have the power to choose, they don't always choose wisely. We must choose for them.

CONNECTION SECTION

Up to this point you've been focusing on your personal use of technology. I still want you to keep that in mind, but I'd like to think about your kids. If you don't have any children at present, you may in the future. If your children are younger, it's not a bad time to think about what's coming down the road and how you're going to react and respond to the pressures you'll face to get your kids the latest and greatest. If you're in the throes of adolescent parenting right now, you'll definitely want to consider all the ways technology is interacting with your kids. (For those of you with younger children or teens, I encourage you to get a copy of my book *The Stranger in Your House*, which deals with how to cope with adolescence. It was written specifically with you in mind—and as someone right there with you I can say, may the Lord have mercy on us all!)

According to the Kaiser Family Foundation study, kids spend almost eleven hours per day multitasking in media. How much time does your child spend with each of the following during the average week?

- Television
- Internet
- Social networking
- DVDs
- Cell phone
- iPod or MP3s
- Game systems

Compare this amount of time with how long you observe your child dealing with schoolwork. The Kaiser Family Foundation study showed that the more media kids used, the lower their academic grades. It's easy to understand: what would a twelve-year-old rather do, write a three-part essay for English or subdue an alien race on the planet Zartha? When kids have the power to choose, they don't always choose wisely. We must choose for them.

Compare the amount of time your kids spend interacting with media each week to how long they spend interacting with you. I must caution you here that interacting does not mean *in the same room* because, with technology, people can be together in the same room and have little or no personal interaction. In the Barna study, the third conclusion they came to was this: we are very connected, but perhaps to people who are not in the room.[8] If you spend an hour with your child while you are watching television and your child is busy texting or on Facebook, you are not spending time *with* each other: you are merely spending time *near* each other. They're not the same, and the latter doesn't count toward the time calculation for this exercise.

Of all the devices you have, do you know how each one operates? Are there any you rely on your child to help you with on a regular basis? Of all the devices your child has, do you know how each one of them operates? How much time have you invested in getting to know what it does, how it works, and thinking about its possible implications? If the amount of time you've spent learning your kids' devices is less than the time it took to buy it, wrap it, and give it, you might want to consider becoming more familiar with it yourself.

Looking at your technology use and the technology your children use, what are three negative consequences that you've personally experienced? What are three positive consequences you've personally experienced? After reading this chapter, what are three changes you believe would turn some of those negatives into positives?

If the amount of time you've spent learning your kids' devices is less than the time it took to buy it, wrap it, and give it, you might want to consider becoming more familiar with it yourself.

It's really all about power. As a parent, especially the parent of a preteen or adolescent, you can feel that transfer of power happening on a nearly daily basis. Some of that transfer is normal, natural, and not bad at all. It *needs* to happen for your child to travel the road of maturity into adulthood. I just want you to be cognizant that technology can accelerate the pace of that transfer because of how powerful and alluring it is and how amazingly in sync so many of our kids are with technology. And be aware that when it comes to technology, our children are mirrors, reflecting our own values, concerns, and priorities.

Chapter 10

WHO ARE YOU, REALLY?

BRYAN NEEDED AN excuse—a good one. Everyone was expecting him to show up for the reunion. As much as he wanted to go, to see people, he was afraid, afraid the Bryan he was in person couldn't possibly compete with the Bryan he'd crafted online. It had taken a great deal of time and effort to create and maintain the online Bryan. He analyzed each picture posted and spent hours researching current events, all to sprinkle his comments with newsworthy nuggets. People who hadn't given him the time of day in school regularly kept in touch now and posted comments on his wall. He hadn't been worth their time then, but he was now. But he was afraid all that would end once he showed up in person. He just hadn't found a way to get out of actually going to the reunion.

He was afraid, afraid the Bryan he was in person couldn't possibly compete with the Bryan he'd crafted online.

If he said he wasn't going too early, he was afraid their attention would wane or stop altogether because he'd no longer be part of the group who was going. Bryan wasn't exactly sure how much of the attention belonged to him personally and how much was just being part of the reunion crowd. No, he would need to wait until the very last minute, giving every indication he was going but then have some sort of flight snafu explain his failure to show. Maybe he could even go to the airport and take a picture of himself behind some big line or take a picture of a parked jet on the tarmac and claim it was his flight, with engine trouble or something.

If that was too elaborate, he might use some sort of work emergency. He'd posted the nature of his work before, with all the requisite embellishments to make it sound more important than it actually was, but he never mentioned a specific company, so there'd be no way to track anything down. He could say there was a computer glitch or project problem that canceled his plans at the final hour. Whatever excuse he used, it would need to cover at least two days because there was the reunion itself on Friday night and then the family picnic on Saturday. He'd need to keep the imaginary problem within the realm of the possible, given the story he'd woven about his work, in case anyone asked questions.

The more he thought about it, the more Bryan hated to miss being on-scene, but it just wasn't worth the risk. It was much safer to live his life filtered through the Internet, where he had control. He could still read about the reunion from those who went and watch for their posts, videos, and photos. After all, that was almost as good as being there. He'd still be able to make witty comments and tag photos but could avoid being in any of them himself. He was used to the observer role, having previously watched the social circles in school from a distance, never being let in. It was safer this way: he couldn't disappoint others, and they were less likely to disappoint him or worse, reject him. Sure, experiencing the reunion online would be a little more artificial and a little less authentic, but all things considered, Bryan found that an acceptable compromise. With that decided, the only thing left was to manufacture his excuse.

GIVING GROUND

Compromise is an interesting word; it can be positive or negative. In the positive vein, it can mean two sides coming together and mutually giving ground in order to meet somewhere in the middle. In the negative, it can mean relinquishing some valuable part of who you are, like your principles or values, and ceding that to someone else. A compromise can also be called a concession, where you give up something in order to reach an accommodation with something or someone you're in conflict with. To reach a compromise or to make a concession requires one or both sides to give up some amount of power and control. The necessity of having to compromise or concede indicates some sort of conflict. Without conflict, where is the need to compromise? Without conflict, why concede?

Technology should assist us in communicating who we are, not distort or overshadow who we are.

In the last chapter we talked about the role technology plays in the transfer of power from one generation to another, especially where parents and kids are concerned. In this chapter I'd like to talk about the transfer of power that takes place when we bind our identities too tightly to this technology. Technology should assist us in communicating who we are, not distort or overshadow who we are. We should be in charge of the technology we use and not find ourselves compromising or conceding our values and principles—our "ground."

People who are comfortable with themselves don't feel compelled to rush out and buy the latest gadget or toy in order to enhance their sense of self.

When we are at peace with who we are, we immunize ourselves from the power of technology to reshape and overtake our lives. The difficulty with technology is that it is powerful enough to create and exacerbate internal conflicts. These internal conflicts can then cause us to begin to compromise what we know to be true and who we are. Then it tempts us to concede to the negative sides of our personalities and the raucous clamor of the world and its values. As Christians, these compromises and concessions cause us to give ground to culture in ways that do not honor God or allow us any peace.

Technology as Magnifier

Because technology allows me a great deal of personal control to do things easily and quickly, I can arrive at places I shouldn't be in record time. Technology has a way of magnifying a person's worst traits and impulses. Paradoxically, we use technology as a way to control and manipulate the image we communicate to others, but how we use technology also broadcasts intimate aspects of our personality, some of which we'd probably rather keep hidden.

For example, people who are obsessed with technology, who believe it confers social status to own the latest and greatest, reveal an underlying lack of self-esteem. People who are comfortable with themselves don't feel compelled to rush out and buy the latest gadget or toy in order to enhance their sense of self. Of course, this propensity didn't always manifest itself with technology; it used to be stereo equipment or cars, designer or brand-name clothing, boats or high-definition LCD TVs. Technology is just the latest

Who You Are Matters

Social media sites have responded to the widespread sense of anonymity online by requiring users to provide real names and to have real off-line identities before granting profile status. Facebook, Twitter, and Google have all summarily deactivated seemingly fake accounts where online handles or pseudonyms obscure real-world identities. Unfortunately, this has sometimes hampered civil discourse as victims and protestors lose a protected, anonymous platform for decrying injustice.

This emphasis on real-world identity has increased users' sense of trust and is welcomed by child-safety advocates, but shifting privacy settings erode user trust and prevent children from going online anonymously, ironically making them even more vulnerable to predators and, now, identity theft.

"Yet," one writer notes, "the full implications of being associated online with a single, real-world identity are only dimly understood. [Fred Stutzman, a fellow at Pittsburgh's Carnegie Mellon University and a researcher in online activity], along with two other researchers, recently conducted an experiment that demonstrated the uses to which the information could be put. Armed with anonymous pictures of volunteers, the researchers were able to use facial recognition software to identify one-third of the subjects by linking to their public Facebook profiles. They were also able to uncover a wealth of other information such as the subjects' personal interests and, in some cases, parts of their social security numbers."[1]

Who you are matters, not only to you and those who love you, but to the people who want access to your data and money as well.

high-priced class symbol broadcasting your inner conflicts, revealing that your sense of self-worth is tied to what you have instead of who you are.

Type A people walked the earth long before technology took such a quantum leap in personal devices. High-strung, nervous controllers always found ways in the past to have their hand in twenty things at once; technology has just made it that much easier. People whose sense of self is tied to what they do instead of who they are have always been susceptible to the lure of saying yes to too many things. With the connectivity and amazing reach of technology, it's just easier to reach out and snatch more balls to juggle. People who keep snatching and juggling more and more balls can certainly put on a great show. But at some point the show becomes uncomfortable as they juggle more balls and leap through more hoops. The question comes to mind, *why are they trying to do so much?* The answer is they need to keep up such a crazy pace in order to feel worthy and valuable as a person—again, their use of technology reveals the inner conflict that their value is derived by what they do instead of who they are.

There have always been activities that could hook you, snare you, and take control of your life. Some of these were illegal, and many were at least frowned upon in years past but not so much anymore. The anonymity of technology has blown accountability out of the water. Never before has it been easier to secretly compromise and engage in behaviors you know are wrong or harmful. When you're the only one enforcing the rules and setting boundaries, it becomes much easier to keep adjusting and moving those lines. However, the more you move the lines and the farther out-of-bounds your behavior becomes, the more likely others will see. When the truth finally surfaces (and it nearly always does, at the most inconvenient opportunity), it can be devastating to come face-to-face with who you've become, what you were willing to compromise, and how much you were willing to concede.

Technology is a willing accomplice in hiding the real you and projecting the false you.

People have always been able to manipulate their image. You could do it with material goods and "conspicuous consumption," or with fashion, cosmetics, and plastic surgery. You could do it through what you wrote, how you spoke, and in how you presented yourself. People have always had difficulty truly liking who they are; they are fearful of rejection. Before the rise of online technology, frequent social contact made it harder to hide. Now, though, it's possible to have virtual communities where you never actually see or hear the other person. They can't hear the trembling lie in your voice or see your fidgety discomfort. They have to take you at face value—without ever seeing your face beyond the pictures you carefully post. Now you can hide in plain sight and spend a great deal of time and energy pretending you have hundreds of friends who are satisfied with the image you project because it's just easier that way. Technology is a willing accomplice in hiding the real you and projecting the false you.

When technology becomes an accomplice to maintaining a lie, you tie yourself even more tightly to it.

THE REFLECTION OF DISCONTENT

I'm not sure anything reveals an inner state of profound discontentment and sheer impatience more than how we use technology.

Technology promises control and heightens expectations. It does all of this in a sort of magical way, because so many people are truly clueless about how technology works. As science fiction author and scientist Arthur C. Clarke once famously wrote, "Any sufficiently advanced technology is indistinguishable from magic."[2] It is the perfect vehicle for late-night ads and infomercial claims; we believe in its infallibility. Technology has become the smoke and mirrors we've come to rely upon to navigate our lives, but, like smoke and mirrors, technology can be elusive and unreliable. When it doesn't work the way we think it should, we can get pretty angry.

I vividly remember when the late Steve Jobs, founder and CEO of Apple, Inc., announced the 4G iPhone and couldn't get the WiFi to work for his demo. This man was the brain behind some amazing technology, and when he desperately needed it to work, it didn't. Of course, being smart, he got the connection running again, but it took a considerable amount of time (and embarrassment) to do so. His discontentment with the failure was evident in his voice and demeanor.

"Any sufficiently advanced technology is indistinguishable from magic." —Arthur C. Clarke

---

I recognized that tone of voice and the demeanor; I've experienced the very same thing when whatever device I was trying to use didn't work as I expected. Having technology that's supposed to work not do its job is like throwing a lit match on a kerosene-soaked barbecue of impatience: it can flare up spectacularly. I've contemplated this matter of why people have such a short fuse for technology that fails them. I believe part of it has to do with unrealized expectations.

We expect technology to work because it does so much of the time.

Because we don't truly understand how technology works, we flounder when it doesn't, unsure of what to do to fix it.

Because we don't know why it isn't working, we have no way of knowing when it will start working, leaving us in an uncomfortable state of tech-less limbo.

When technology doesn't work and we can't do anything to fix it, we tap into feelings of anger and frustration, of being out of control of something we believe is vital to our well-being.

When did we surrender that much power to inanimate objects, allowing them to wreak such havoc in our lives? It's as if we really do want to believe in fairy tales and have decided technology is our surrogate happy ending. When we have our technology, we will live happily ever after.

We have tied technology to personal happiness, which is unwise. Happiness in life should never be based on external circumstances. Other people and outside circumstances, like technology, are erratic and unreliable. Instead, personal happiness ought to be anchored to something more solid, reliable, and trustworthy.

The more reliant we become on technology, the more control over our personal happiness we cede to it, the more power we transfer to it. The more power we transfer to it, the more we expect to receive in the bargain and the more discontent and unhappiness we experience when that bargain doesn't meet our expectations.

Technology can act as both a mirror and magnifier for our personality traits, whether good or bad. You may seek to control how others perceive you through technology, but how you use it actually projects your own fears and compulsions, your preferences and priorities to a very broad community. What you use and how you use it tell others what you secretly believe about yourself.

In a perverse paradox, I buy technology to enhance my life, but without care, that same technology can quickly degrade my life to its worst forms of self-expression.

- I buy a cell phone in order to stay better connected to my family but end up using that same cell phone to interrupt my family time.

- I give my kids a cell phone and tell them it's so I can always get hold of them but then neglect them in person.

- I try to teach my kids that stuff doesn't matter, but before I know it, I've bought them more stuff than they know what to do with.

- I use technology as a way to be more time efficient, to buy myself time, but I find myself even more impatient with every new gadget.

- I use technology as a way to be more time efficient but find myself using that "extra" time to use more technology for what I want to do.

- I stay connected all the time so I won't have to worry, but I end up worrying all the time anyway.

- I use technology to stay in touch with family and friends, to build relationships, but I find myself tempted to "tweak" my communications to my advantage.

I buy technology to enhance my life, but without care, that same technology can quickly degrade my life to its worst forms of self-expression.

Technology has a way of putting me in the driver's seat of my life. When I'm in total control, what does it say about who I am? What does it say about my priorities, my character? Is that truly who I want to be?

CONNECTION SECTION

In some ways I think our use of technology can be like certain people out walking their dog. There may be a leash involved, but it appears the dog is using it to drag the owner along. The owner is tethered to the dog, and the dog is in control. When the dog wants to go, the owner runs behind, huffing and puffing to keep up, struggling to keep their arm from being pulled out of its socket. When the dog wants to stop, the owner is forced to brake suddenly to avoid tripping and falling over the dog. As long as the dog wants to stop and sniff, there is no going forward. It's quite easy to see who's in control, regardless of who's holding the leash.

You can think you have your technology use leashed, but do you really? Are you in control of your technology, or is it dragging you down a path you don't want to go? Who are you with your technology? What does your technology use reveal about you?

Any time a behavior gets out of control, there is a reason. Consider the following reasons and how they may be affecting your technology choices:

- *Pleasure-seeking:* This is so true of devices like game consoles, but it can also be true when experiencing the "hit" of getting a new message or finding a novel factoid. Remember, these devices act on your brain and nervous system. They can become a way you reward yourself for the stresses in your life.

- *Discomfort-avoidance:* These devices have an amazing ability to distract. Like comfort food, technology can be used to numb negative emotions such as loneliness, boredom, or frustration. You can find yourself engaging in these activities not because they are positive and healthy but because they put off dealing with things you find negative.

- *Fear:* Staying connected to these devices can become a survival tactic, a way to know what's happening so you can exert control over your life. You connect, not necessarily to enjoy the positive, but so you can mitigate and control a feeling of fear. These fears can be broad-based:

  - Fear of the loss of significance if you don't continue to maintain an online presence

  - Fear of loss of control if you don't have input into every possible situation

  - Fear of guilt if you miss something important or fail to meet someone else's expectations

  - Fear of rejection and loss of status if you aren't up-to-date on the latest and greatest

You might think the above would go under the category of control issues, but I think they're actually fear issues. The only things we attempt to control are those things we truly fear. The more fearful we are, the harder we try to control.

As you think about the devices you use and how you use them, I want you to do so through the filters of pleasure seeking, discomfort avoidance, and fear. Be very specific about what you're doing and why. Come clean with yourself about the underlying reasons.

This exercise isn't meant to make you feel worse about yourself but to awaken you to what truly motivates you. These motivations are what bring you back time and again to these devices and behaviors. These motivations are the rationalizations you use when justifying why you need to check your e-mail every five minutes, why you must go online each night for several hours, or why you should immediately answer every call or text on your cell phone.

The only things we attempt to control are those things we truly fear. The more fearful we are, the harder we try to control.

These motivations have a way of defining who you think you are. When who you think you are is defined by your fears, failures, and weaknesses, it can be difficult to find the courage and strength to change for the better. Before you can truly fight for a different identity, you need to know what you honestly believe about yourself.

You need to know: Are you walking the dog, or is the dog walking you?

Chapter 11

FIND THE OFF SWITCH

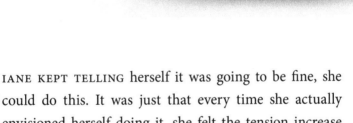

DIANE KEPT TELLING herself it was going to be fine, she could do this. It was just that every time she actually envisioned herself doing it, she felt the tension increase and heard a multitude of doomsday prophecies screaming in her head. No, she could do this; she *would* do this.

She was headed to South America for a long-overdue second honeymoon with her husband, two weeks off the grid. She wasn't going totally "dark" because she couldn't imagine not being able to contact the kids, so she had subscribed to a one-month international plan with her mobile provider. The cost had been pretty steep—not for the access, but for the per-minute charges—but she knew she could be disciplined while on the road and would use it only for emergencies. Bill, nervous about the cost, had given her a very short list of what he considered an emergency, something just south of an act of God. And he'd squarely rejected any work issue as being even remotely considered an emergency. However, Diane had made it clear that, if necessary, her work could call her; she'd just expense the charges. Having that option, at least, made her feel better.

Overall, Diane found it strange that she needed to feel better about going on a trip she'd been anticipating for years. She and Bill had been planning this since the kids were little, and now they finally had the financial means to pull it off. But Diane hadn't anticipated realizing how dependent she'd become on all this technology and how truly apprehensive she was about living for two weeks without it. What if there was a problem with the dogs at the kennel? What if there was a problem at the house? What if something happened to one of the family while they were gone? Of course, realistically she couldn't do anything about it, but she wanted to know immediately. It was the not knowing about what might happen that gave her the funny, uneasy feeling in the pit of her stomach and cast a pall over her excitement at the trip.

While she and Bill were planning the trip, all they could talk about was how good it would be to get away from everything. Now that it was finally here, getting away from everything didn't feel so great. Well, if necessary, they could always find a major city with an Internet café, and she did have her cell phone. The whole point of the trip was to be together and relax. She and Bill would be together, and knowing she could get online if absolutely necessary would help her relax.

Going off the grid for two weeks was like walking a tightrope; being able to connect if needed was just a personal safety net. If she didn't overdo it, Bill would be fine. She would be fine.

She could do this, Diane assured herself for the hundredth time.

THE OFF SWITCH

The other day there was a problem with the copier at work. Something wasn't operating properly, and when we called the tech, we were told to power the machine off and turn it back on again, sort of a reboot. The weird thing was, none of us could figure out where the off switch was. The copier is literally on all the time, 24/7. We had to ask the tech about the off switch and felt pretty dumb doing so.

Every piece of technology has an off switch, whether we know where it is or not, whether we want to use it or not.

The same sort of thing happened the first time I flew in an airplane after getting my new cell phone. Of all the things I'd figured out how to do on the phone, it didn't dawn on me to find out how to turn the thing off, totally off. Up to that point I'd never done it. Sure, I'd put it on silent and knew about the airplane mode, but I'd never turned it completely off. Luckily there was someone younger sitting next to me who knew how to operate my phone.

Every piece of technology has an off switch, whether we know where it is or not, whether we want to use it or not. The answer to whether or not you genuinely want to use the off switch is to actually use it. It's one of life's enduring ironies that things we use to exert control often have a way of biting us back. Technology allows us to arrange the world so we can control it, but it has the real potential to turn on us. Then we end up becoming controlled by the very technology we employed to give us control. It's the classic bite-back of addiction: we end up a slave to what we use to master our world.

Perhaps *slave* seems like a harsh word, but think about the voluntary enslavement you either see or experience on a regular basis where technology is concerned. It's getting out of a meeting, and before you've even left the room, you're immediately viewing calls and downloading e-mail to your smartphone as you're walking. It's that edge of anxiety if you can't log in and see what's going on, risking being out of the loop. It's telling yourself you'll log on only to check messages, only to finish up over an hour later—and late to whatever activity had the audacity to intrude. It was supposed to be about you having access to everything, but you found out it was about everything having access to you. Control has a way of switching sides if we're not careful.

Tech Detox

So, how do you know if you've crossed over that line from use to obsession, from controller to being controlled? Perhaps the true answer to whether or not you have control over the technology in your life is to do a tech detox. Detox is a shortened version of the word *detoxification*, which is common in the medical world. A medical detoxification removes harmful substances that have built up in the body. It's often used for people coming off of alcohol or drug addiction, whose bodies are so toxic due to those substances they need to be medically cleansed in order to restore physical health.

There can be significant toxic effects of shame and guilt when your use of technology undermines your values, morals, principles, and priorities, haunting you even when you're not online.

It can be hard to accept that the technology we use every day may be building up toxic by-products in our lives:

- There is ongoing research that suggests that cell phone use may contribute to cancer. The World Health Organization now classifies cell phone use under the same category as lead, engine exhaust, and chloroform, under "carcinogenic hazard."[1]

- Technology contributes to the propensity to multitask, creating heightened levels of stress. Stress is a known factor in a variety of negative health impacts, from heart disease, to stroke, to obesity, to high blood pressure.

- The use of technology can be toxic to your relationships when time with technology is chosen over time with family and friends.

- There can be significant toxic effects of shame and guilt when your use of technology undermines your values, morals, principles, and priorities, haunting you even when you're not online.

- Technology can often mean a sedentary lifestyle, opting to experience life online as opposed to outdoors. An inactive, sedentary lifestyle has significant toxic effects on your health and mental well-being.

- When you don't spend time with yourself, using technology to distract from difficult thoughts, those unresolved feelings and truncated contemplation build up in the recesses of your mind, often finding inappropriate ways of release.

As much as it may pain you to consider this, it could be time for a tech detox, a voluntary reduction in your use of technology. It means willingly giving up something you've come to rely on. The more things you're hooked into, the harder this will be and the more anxiety it will produce. However, when conducted in a thoughtful, prepared manner, a tech detox can help you release some of the negative buildup of your technology use and give you the break you need to make better choices going forward.

Here's how I recommend approaching this:

Plan your progress. Technology is so much a part of our lives, you'll need to be intentional about what you're going to give up, for what reason, and for how long. This isn't something you can do haphazardly, or you'll just end up reverting back to old habits. The key word here is *intentional.* You want to go into this with eyes wide open so you can monitor and respond to your responses and reactions to digital deprivation. Develop a plan, and then stick to it. This will help you weather the squalls of anxiety that can threaten to overturn your best intentions.

Give yourself permission to spend the next few hours concentrating on just one thing—enjoying the movie with your family or the game with your kids.

Start small with a digital break. Some of you may consider a tech detox as a sort of digital diet and cringe at the concept, thinking you're going to have to do the cyber equivalent of never having another piece of chocolate cake while living on tofu and grapefruit ad nauseum. Relax—those kinds of diets don't work with food, and I doubt they'd work for technology either. Instead, what I propose is that you start with a baby step. For example, if you're going to go see a movie with your family or attend one of your kids' soccer games, leave your cell phone in the car. Give yourself permission to spend the next few hours concentrating on just one thing—enjoying the movie with your family or the game with your kids.

If you're the kind of person who needs to check e-mail every fifteen minutes, don't. Give yourself permission to check it less frequently, say, every hour. If you already only check it every hour, try checking it just three or four times a day. The point is, you are desensitizing yourself to the panic involved with a reduction in frequency of the behavior. Start small and allow yourself to experience incremental victories.

Think about all of the tech devices you use every day—when,

> **Dr. Weil's Data Smog Diet**
>
> Andrew Weil, MD, has instituted a simple set of personal rules that help him defeat information overload and unhealthy stress:
>
> "Deleting, without remorse, all games from my computer and mobile devices."
>
> "Refusing to aimlessly surf the Web. I always have a specific object in mind and resolve to seek only that."
>
> "Handling e-mail almost exclusively on my desktop computer, almost never on my cell phone or notepad. When I leave my office for the day, usually in the afternoon, I leave the computer and e-mail behind until morning."
>
> Weil reports that he is much happier having made these changes. "My mind is clearer, my attention span longer and my real (as opposed to virtual) friendships closer."[2]

where, and how. Identify an area you can decrease; then determine what amount of time feels doable. Again, start small, but be consistent over the amount of time you've determined for the detox. Make a list of all the tech things you use and rank them from easiest to hardest. Start with the easiest first and work your way down the list.

Don't just reduce or remove; replace. When you decide to stop doing something, especially something you enjoy, you create a void. Whatever you were doing filled some sort of need, and ceasing that activity will cause that need to resurface. If you don't fill that need, that void, with something else, it's going to feel like an enormous black hole, sucking all your resolve down its dark maw. Be proactive; as you decide what you're going to reduce, determine something positive, healthy, and uplifting you're going to replace it with.

Suppose you decide you're going to reduce your amount of Facebook time during the week, from daily to only every other day. On those non-Facebook days, you could arrange to meet in person with a friend and go for a walk or meet for coffee and old-fashioned conversation. You could get out and let the dog walk you, or you could window-shop with a family member. You could finally tackle clearing out that extra bedroom or painting the hall. If you're filling up the time with something good, doing without the digital won't seem so bad.

One of the objectives of a tech detox is to discover just how far this whole technology thing has gone in your life. But there has to be more to it than that. The more-to-it generally comes down to what has been missing in your life as a concession to all the technology. Is it spending time outside? Is it spending time with others? Is it spending time alone, just you and no technological white noise? Technology and your use of it have crowded out other valuable things in your life. While you're saying no to whatever the gadget or habit is, say yes to what's been missing. Don't just clear out the one without inviting in the other.

Clarify your goals. Along those same lines, you'll want to be specific about why you're doing the detox. Write down your goals, and then shorten them to quick, memorable phrases you can repeat to yourself when the going gets tough and you're tempted to google the latest gossip. Using technology can be fun and entertaining, both very positive outcomes. In order to reduce your use, it's important for you to firmly fix on the greater good you're trying to achieve through your controlled use. Yes, spending dinnertime texting to friends is fun and entertaining, but giving your family priority with your presence and undivided attention is the greater good.

Be clear on the detox rules, and stick to them. Decide beforehand what the parameters of your detox are going to be. If you decide not to check work e-mails from home in the evening, specify the hours you *can* check them. The more specific the parameters, the less room there will be for cheating. Don't cheat. Just because you made the rules doesn't mean you get to break them. This is also why it's important to start small; the fewer the rules, the easier it will be to keep them. Then, as you rack up the victories, you can expand the rules. As you gain successes, the first rules will seem less like "rules" and will feel more natural, less restrictive, and normal.

While you're saying no to whatever the gadget or habit is, say yes to what's been missing. Don't just clear out the one without inviting in the other.

Determine the consequences ahead of time. You don't want to cheat, but at some point you probably will. When you're planning your detox, plan for failure. Decide ahead of time how you're going to reset your detox when you answer that call during the school play or smuggle your phone into your luggage during your weekend away. I couldn't begin to calculate the number of diets that went belly-up by impulsively giving in to that cookie or candy bar. It's as if there was some fine print in your contract with yourself that said you either had to adhere to your rules perfectly or all bets were off. Nobody is perfect, and you won't keep your convictions perfectly, so give yourself a break. Know a side trip is coming, and provide yourself a way back to the straight and narrow.

Take advantage of what you've learned. The goal should not be merely to see how long you do something, to prove mastery over it, knowing you're just going to dive back into it with renewed passion, enthusiasm, and a great sigh of relief. One goal of a tech detox should be to learn that you can actually live without it, but that's not the only goal. You should also strive to use a tech detox to learn more about yourself and how you interact with technology in all aspects of your being, what I call the whole person: emotionally, relationally, physically, and spiritually. By paying attention to each of these areas during a tech detox, you can learn how technology is truly useful to you in each area and how it's actually harmful.

Take the next step. Armed with the knowledge you've gained about yourself and your tech use, establish new boundaries. Whenever you are confronted with something new, move from knowledge to application. Knowledge is not enough to modify behavior; you must apply what you've learned in order to change patterns. Learning is like growing; if you stop, you atrophy. Take what you've learned and keep growing; keep moving toward positive and healthy integration of technology in your life. Technology is always changing, and you need to keep moving and to stay flexible in order to keep up without being controlled again.

A tech detox doesn't have to be difficult. It's an exercise in self-discipline, which ultimately is an exercise in self-enlightenment.

Knowledge is not enough to modify behavior; you must apply what you've learned in order to change patterns.

FAMILY DETOX

Some of you reading this live alone, but many of you will be part of a larger family unit, where each person's use of technology intersects and affects the others. While there is a place for a personal tech detox, there is certainly also a place for a family tech detox. You may want to begin first by trying out the tech detox yourself before evangelizing it to the family. Who knows? Your results may be so impressive it may influence others to join you (or not—especially if you have teenagers). But when you begin to take your family on this journey, don't let a lack of enthusiasm or even outright derision stop you from working toward the goal.

The steps are very similar to a personal tech detox.

Plan your progress. When it was just you, planning was simpler. But in order to implement a family tech detox, you'll need to include the entire family in the planning process. This means you'll need to be prepared to move to the positive side of compromise and not concede to your twelve-year-old who cannot imagine life without texting for a week. Are you the parent? Yes. You could just demand everyone take part (and you may have to), but hopefully you can encourage others to buy into the detox. As a way to plan, prior to the family meeting, you could note how, when, and how long those in your family use technology, including you and any other adults. If you can show evidence of the large amounts of time being spent on various devices, it may be easier for you to gain agreement.

Start small with a digital break. Be prepared to discuss the difference between your definition of small and other family members' definitions of small. As a way to start small, you may ask every family member to self-designate a reduction in use and jointly come up with an activity to reduce that affects the entire family. For example, one family member may limit texting to one hour per day. Another may limit computer games to one hour per day. Another may agree to restrict work e-mails to one hour per day. Then the entire family may agree to a no-tech zone during dinner. Allow each family member to offer his or her contribution to the tech detox, and work together to come up with an acceptable joint restriction.

> ## Ask every family member to self-designate a reduction in use and jointly come up with an activity to reduce that affects the entire family.

Don't just reduce or remove; replace. Help each family member come up with not only a reduction or a removal but also a replacement activity. Ideally, these should include family time and activities instead of reverting to self-isolating choices. The family member who is reducing the amount of text time could replace it with watching a DVD with others. The one who is reducing gaming time could go to a local park to physically play a game with others. The family member who agreed to restrict work e-mails could help with a household chore or errand. For the no-tech zone at dinner, this would mean no television, music, or other distractions, just time to talk and be together. (If a quiet dinner feels awkward at first, that's fine. You don't need to "fix" it. Just stick with the rules and allow conversation to thaw naturally.) During the detox, choose a night, if you're able, and go out to a favorite local restaurant for dinner as a change of pace.

Clarify your goals. You'll need to jointly clarify individual goals and family goals for your family tech detox. Just because you're the driving force behind this, your family will not let you off of the hook for your own tech use. Some of the goals your family comes up with may directly affect you, especially for some of those behaviors and devices you've placed farther down your "difficulty" list.

Just as with the personal detox, try to articulate the agreed-upon goals as pithy, memorable phrases so you can encourage each other with why you're doing this in the first place. Make a list of these goals and attach it to the refrigerator so everyone can see them and be reminded.

Be clear on the detox rules, and stick to them. Remember the part about cheating on your personal tech detox? Well, there are more people involved now who will be delighted to call you out if you cheat. Because you are the one setting this in motion, you're going to come under intense scrutiny, and any cheating on your part could be used as an excuse to cheat by others. That's why it might be beneficial for you to start with a personal tech detox first and then bring in the rest of the family when you feel strong enough to maintain a steady example.

You'll also want to be in agreement with any other adults in the family. It will be difficult to pull this off if you're steadfastly adhering to the rules but other adults undermine you. It would be like if everyone agreed to refrain from eating Hostess snack cakes, but then someone regularly devours Ding Dongs all around the house. Not good. I'm not saying you can't still do this, but you may need to modify your family restrictions to maximize success for more recalcitrant adults. You may need to work with that adult privately to come to some sort of agreement on how to handle his or her behavior in front of the rest of the family.

The best thing to do, in any situation, is to have the rules clearly agreed upon and understood by all. The rules could also be written up and posted on the fridge next to the goals.

Determine the consequences ahead of time. Because there are multiple people involved, you'll want to have agreement on what the consequences will be and who will enforce them. Allow other family members to make suggestions first and hold your own opinion until last; you may be surprised at how reasonable others can be. Whenever possible, agree to what others suggest, because if you have to dispense consequences, having them come from others will make them less identifiable with you. Make sure you include yourself in the group and don't hold yourself apart, like some sort of super-arbiter. If there is a breach in the rules, bring everyone back together to deal with it.

It will be difficult to pull this off if you're steadfastly adhering to the rules but other adults undermine you.

Take advantage of what you've learned. Each family member will, of course, be responsible to take the lessons learned from this family tech detox and put them into practice. However, you can learn a great deal about each family member and the collective family through this kind of shared experience. Because the tech detox will often be front and center in the minds of your family, you have a built-in conversation starter. You could touch base with each person during dinner or at another joint family time to gather feedback and share insights. Plan to come together at the end of your family tech detox for a family debrief.

Take the next step. As part of your family detox debrief, encourage each family member to move from knowledge to application. Ask each one to think of ways to take what was learned and put it into practice with each person's use of technology. As a parent, you may want to use this as an opportunity to either reinforce or institute a family guideline around a particular activity or device; that is your prerogative as a parent. Realize that this discussion does not need to end when the family detox does. You can use this experience in the future when another technology is introduced.

CONNECTION SECTION

"Technology is the knack of so arranging the world that we don't have to experience it."[3]

So said the Swiss novelist and author Max Frisch. He died in 1991, which was the dark ages as far as our current technology goes, but I believe he was correct. Technology certainly is ubiquitous and has its place, but it should never serve as a substitute for experiencing real life, good or bad. All of these amazing ways to connect to technology should never replace connecting with people, especially your family and loved ones.

Never have we been able to escape into a more compelling artificial reality than today, and that artificiality is only going to become even more compelling in the future. Each of us only has a set amount of time on this earth to experience life. Life needs to be *experienced* to be truly lived. I don't want to live a half-life, enmeshed in an artificial world. I don't want my family to settle for less than real life. I don't want that to happen, but with all of the technology in my life and what's coming my way, I need to be constantly on guard. One way to stay alert and aware is to periodically disconnect and pay attention to how I feel, what I think, and what I do in response. My hope is you'll take the time to do just that, first with a personal tech detox and then, if applicable, with a family tech detox.

For this Connection Section, I'd like you to begin to look at what a personal tech detox would look like for you:

- What are you going to reduce, and for how long?

- What activity are you going to replace it with?

- Why that activity? What need are you filling with the replacement?

- What are your goals for this tech detox?

- What will your rules be, and how are you going to increase your ability to stick to them?

- If you fail, what will you do? How will you get back on track?

- How will you keep track of what you're learning during this time? How will be sure to capture your thoughts and feelings?

- Once you've completed this personal tech detox, how will you determine your next step?

Life needs to be experienced to be truly lived. I don't want to live a half-life, enmeshed in an artificial world.

I encourage you not to make this a head-knowledge exercise of *what would I do if?* Don't just imagine yourself doing this; please do it. Use the steps I've outlined, think about it, start small, and be intentional. You don't have to go and live in a hut in the woods to gain insight and realize value from a tech detox. Start with something you can do and then do it. Then use that success to motivate you to take another risk.

Really listen to yourself through the process. One of the most important voices drowned out in this distracting technological maelstrom is your own.

Chapter 12

THE ULTIMATE FILTER

I ENDED THE LAST chapter by saying, "One of the most important voices drowned out in this distracting technological maelstrom is your own." There is another voice that gets drowned out by technology if we're not careful, and that is God's voice. I purposely waited to present a scriptural perspective on the subject of our use of technology until the end so that God, as it were, could have the final say. His Word is always the final word on any subject, as we're reminded in Proverbs 19:21: "Many are the plans in a man's heart, but it is the LORD's purpose that prevails."

So I guess you could call this the God chapter. For this chapter I'm going to continue to tell you what I think, but I'm also going to relate what I've learned and understand about how God thinks, using His Book as a guide, as well as my own experiences as a Christian and as a Christian therapist. Many of you reading this book will also have a faith, a belief in God. Some of you may not have any faith, or perhaps your faith has taken a beating over the years; it's still there, but it's tattered and threadbare.

Even if you feel shaky in the faith-in-God department, I invite you to stick with me and read through this chapter anyway. I believe there is still wisdom to gain and lessons to learn regardless of where you land on faith; you can always ascribe these lessons to common sense, moral teachings, or shared values. If you've never contemplated a personal faith in God up to this point in your life, read on, because perhaps you will—if not today, then maybe tomorrow. If your faith is a bit tattered at this point in your life, read on; perhaps you'll find material to mend.

Years ago I received some great advice on reading content that contained portions I might disagree with, and it was to read like I was eating fish. I was told to read but "pick out the bones." The admonition was to be careful, but to go ahead and get all the good out of it I could. That's my invitation to you if you're concerned we're not in sync in matters of faith and religion. You've hung in with me for this long; please don't stop now. Just pick out the bones. (You might want to remember, however, that bones have a way of providing structure and framework for things, so while you're picking them out, you may not want to discard them completely.)

Regardless of where you land on faith, you can always ascribe these lessons to common sense, moral teachings, or shared values.

BOXES

We are adept at compartmentalizing our lives. We have a work face and a home face. We act one way with close friends and another way toward clerks in stores or servers in restaurants. Our children know us in ways our coworkers do not, and vice versa. Christians are not immune to compartmentalization. We too can have a work face, a home face, and a separate church face. We can act, speak, and respond one way when stuck in traffic and a completely different way when stuck in church.

Technology is also great for compartmentalizing, at creating discrete little boxes to contain things. We have our work e-mail box and our social network box. We have the who we are in our online box and the who we are in our off-line box. When we interact with different devices, we can physically enter into a sort of boxlike zone. Have you ever watched your kid playing a video game, interrupt your spouse while online, or been interrupted yourself? Technology use can create a distinct "space" around us, one in which we feel in charge, in control, and thoroughly enthralled. We erect signs that say "Don't bother me" or, worse, "You can't see me."

Because we are able to live our lives in separate little compartments, it's tempting to think that God sees or cares about how we act in only some of those boxes. It can be easy to delude ourselves into believing we get to choose which boxes are secret and which ones are accountable to God. That is not, however, the truth. Proverbs 5:21 says, "For a man's ways are in full view of the LORD, and he examines all his paths." Paths, boxes, zones, spaces, compartments—they're all words pointing to the same personal choices. And through all of them, God sees and examines what you and I do with technology. "Nothing in all creation is hidden from God's sight. Everything is uncovered and laid bare before the eyes of him to whom we must give account" (Hebrews 4:13).

Simply put, we are accountable.

LIVING ON THE EDGE

I have a child at home who lives on the edge. He constantly tests the boundaries I set, getting as close to the edge as possible. On my more exasperated days I have trouble viewing this as a positive trait. However, once I get over my initial irritation, I remember that this is my adventurous, spontaneous, carefree child, who bounces up to the edge not out of disrespect but because there's just so much *out there* to do and see. He is the risk taker, the tenacious spirit, the explorer who may one day discover something new and exciting and necessary because he's used to testing the boundaries of "can't."

Boundary testing is life experience, and sometimes more than just the boundary gets bumped and bruised in the process.

Until that day comes, though, my patience is tested every time one of my boundaries is bumped to see if it's still holding, still valid, and still in force. I have a hard time not reverting to an old-fashioned, top-of-the-lungs test of the will. I have a very hard time remembering that probably the reason his behavior is so irritating is because I am this way myself. At least, I am a bit of a boundary bumper with God where technology is concerned. I don't want to be told, "No," "You can't," or "Wait." I love this stuff and tend to race off along the path of technology without looking down for the inevitable pitfalls along the way. This tendency, of course, means

I've fallen on my face a time or two where technology is concerned by getting too enmeshed, too enthralled, and too involved, and I've had to turn around and straighten out my priorities. It's meant I've had to reevaluate what I've given to my kids and what I've allowed them to do with technology. Boundary testing is life experience, and sometimes more than just the boundary gets bumped and bruised in the process.

COUNTING THE COST

Before you and I go running headlong toward the next technological marvel, we may want to consider looking down first and stopping long enough to consider the consequences. Another way to say "consider the consequences" is "count the cost." I've always heard the phrase "count the cost" in conjunction with Luke 14:28, which says, "For which of you, intending to build a tower, does not sit down first and count the cost, whether he has enough to finish it" (NKJV). The lesson is, before you start something, you'd better take time to figure out what you're getting into. A while back, however, while reading through the Old Testament, I ran across a couple other verses that talked about building and cost. The first was Joshua 6:26: "At that time Joshua pronounced this solemn oath: 'Cursed before the LORD is the man who undertakes to rebuild this city, Jericho: At the cost of his firstborn son he will lay its foundations; at the cost of his youngest he will set up its gates."

Joshua sounded a warning about a future pitfall. It's remarkably succinct and specific. Unfortunately his warning went unheeded, for I found this verse further on in 1 Kings 16:34: "In Ahab's time, Hiel of Bethel rebuilt Jericho. He laid its foundations at the cost of his firstborn son Abiram, and he set up its gates at the cost of his youngest son Segub, in accordance with the word of the LORD spoken by Joshua son of Nun." Hiel of Bethel failed to heed the warning. He failed to pay attention to the pitfall. He failed to "count the cost."

I don't know, but I suspect Hiel of Bethel probably did a fine job rebuilding Jericho. He clearly didn't let the death of his firstborn, Abiram, deter him when he laid the city's foundations. He carried on with the reconstruction all the way to finally setting up the gates in their proper places along the rebuilt walls, even despite the death of his youngest son, Segub. It may have been a lovely city to look at, and in the opinion of the people in the region, it was beautiful on the surface, but it hid an ugly truth below. Hiel failed to consider the consequences or count the cost, but he still paid the price, as did his sons.

I need to remember to count the cost where technology is concerned—how I use it myself, what I bring into my home, and how I allow my children to interact with it. I don't want to finish like Hiel, with something beautiful and beneficial to others but that comes at such a ghastly personal price. I need to remember that technology is powerful and can be very dangerous.

No headlong rushes toward the shiny, the new, the latest, and greatest. Instead, I need to stop and consider the consequences first.

I need to think of technology the same way I do a car. I would never allow my kids to operate something as powerful, compelling, and potentially dangerous as a car before they've been trained and are old enough to handle the responsibility. Cars are mixed blessings, as is technology. That little cell phone I bought my son for good has the potential to do harm. I need to count the cost. The game console that he begged and pleaded for at Christmas is fun and engaging, but it has the potential to consume his attention to his detriment. I need to count the cost. That computer in my house that I bought and use and love still has the power to corrupt the innocence of my kids and the integrity of my family. I need to count the cost. I need to count the cost for myself and for those I love. No headlong rushes toward the shiny, the new, the latest, and greatest. Instead, I need to stop and consider the consequences first.

PEACE AND QUIET

In chapter 2 we talked about the crazy and chaotic multi-taxed life that many of us seem to live with or at least flirt with. We talked about trying to juggle too many things at once and living on auto-pilot. We looked at maximizers and sufficers, at type A and type B people. People have always tried to take on too much, to respond to the want-to-have-it-now urges instead of enduring with wait-until-later patience. We get sidetracked by the urgent and forget what's important. We lose our way and end up getting bogged down and trapped in uncomfortable and sometimes dangerous places.

We are such sheep. When frightened, we react as a herd, without regard for where we're headed. Left alone, we wander off and get lost. We spend so much time needlessly struggling, contending, and moving that we forget to simply stop and rest.

Rest is not a concept on friendly terms with the current culture. Rest is something you do at the end of a very long day, when you're so tired or so drugged you can't do anything else—and even then we don't call it rest; we call it sleep. Rest conjures up impossible images of a stress-free snapshot in time, perhaps with warm air, shade, and a cool drink. In our anxiety-laced culture we forget that we were made to rest. In our productivity-driven culture we forget that even God Himself took time to rest and it didn't, somehow, negatively affect His schedule, performance evaluations, or end product. In our shortsightedness we think rest is outdated and forget that rest is timeless.

We are such sheep. When frightened, we react as a herd, without regard for where we're headed. Left alone, we wander off and get lost.

The Bible talks about rest from Genesis to Revelation; the concept saturates Scripture. One of the most-loved passages of all time is a short treatise on this very subject; though written thousands of years ago, describing an agrarian culture and profession few people practice today, Psalm 23 still resonates because people haven't fundamentally changed. Some of you can probably recite it from memory. If so, take a deep breath, close your eyes, and do so. For the rest of us, I'm providing it here for you to read and contemplate:

> The LORD is my shepherd, I shall not be in want.
> He makes me lie down in green pastures,
> he leads me beside quiet waters,
> he restores my soul.
> He guides me in right paths of righteousness
>   for his name's sake.
> Even though I walk
>   through the valley of the shadow of death,
> I will fear no evil,
>   for you are with me;
> your rod and your staff,
>   they comfort me.

You prepare a table before me
    in the presence of my enemies.
You anoint my head with oil;
    my cup overflows.
Surely goodness and love will follow me
    all the days of my life,
and I will dwell in the house of the LORD forever.

God's way is not a whirlwind of craziness; it is sufficient and restful. It is quiet and refreshing. It is supporting and comforting. God's way is not enamored with the latest and newest; it is ancient and eternal. Regardless of where technology takes our culture, we need to learn God's way and adhere to it. We need to surrender our fears and compulsions to God, not join them to technology in a futile attempt to outrun them. Even with technology we can't run fast enough to outpace our fears and compulsions; we can only make them stronger.

It is not possible to do two things at once, no matter how hard we try. The harder we try, the more stress we introduce into our lives and the less rest and peace we experience. God, in Psalm 46:10, says, "Be still, and know that I am God." He invites us to quiet ourselves and contemplate Him. He asks us to mono-task, not multitask, in order to know Him better. This is hard to do; it requires turning down the volume of our lives and calming our frenetic thoughts and activity. It means turning our attention to one thing instead of many.

Choosing quiet means saying no to technology distractions. It means finding a time each day, whenever possible, to intentionally choose to be fully present with God. No cell phone calls, no text bells, no e-mail beeps. No game noise, no television clamor, no Internet banners. Just you, still and quiet, giving God your undivided attention. Did you know you have His? Proverbs 15:3 says,

"The eyes of the LORD are everywhere, keeping watch on the wicked and the good."

Choosing quiet means saying no to technology distractions. It means finding a time each day, whenever possible, to intentionally choose to be fully present with God.

AMERICAN IDOL

At some point in history we stopped worshiping physical idols—at least most of us did. But that doesn't mean we stopped *idol worship;* we just exchanged wood and stone figures for things such as money, fame, and, yes, technology. Writing in 1995, the late Neil Postman—author, media theorist, and cultural critic—said it well when he described how technology has become to us a modern god: "...in the sense that people believe technology works, that they rely on it, that it makes promises, that they are bereft when denied access to it, that they are delighted when they are in its presence, that for most people it works in mysterious ways, that they condemn people who speak against it, that they stand in awe of it, and that, in the born-again mode, they will alter their lifestyles, their schedules, their habits, and their relationships to accommodate it."[1]

It's amazing how much priority, power, and omnipotence we ascribe to our little technological devices. Though they are made by flawed, fallible people, we expect them to operate perfectly every time. We're exasperated when they fail us, but we forgive them readily and immediately try again. We buy them comfortable little cases and shiny accessories. We devote time and energy to them each day and make sure they get tucked up and plugged in each night. It's easy, really, to see why we put such faith in them; they are just so amazing, and we're not terribly sure how they work. We're just glad they do. These techy little devices are well worth their weight in gold; we just no longer fashion that gold into statues.

There is a brutally honest passage about the foolishness of worshiping our own handmade idols in Isaiah 44, particularly in verses 13–20. Isaiah paints a word picture of a carpenter who goes out to cut down a piece of wood. Half of the wood goes into the fire to warm himself and cook his food. With the other half of that same piece of wood the carpenter carves an idol and bows down to it in worship, praying to it to save him. The very thing he had complete control over to burn up, he bows down and prays to. Sounds ridiculous, right?

We need to be careful we're not doing the same thing. With technology we obtain the components and put these devices together to make our lives more comfortable, warm our hearts, and feed our various hungers. Then we act as if we can't live without them; we turn to these man-made devices we've gathered about to "save us"! It was foolish thousands of years ago, and it's no less foolish now, which should be a warning to us because idol worship was extremely prevalent back then. People are still people, and we still do foolish things, so it shouldn't surprise us we're still susceptible to this tendency today.

When we tie our personal happiness and ability to function to technology rather than to God, we elevate technology to idol status. Here's what God, through the apostle Paul, has to say about this age-old pitfall: "No temptation has seized you except what is common to man. And God is faithful; he will not let you be tempted beyond what you can bear. But when you are tempted, he will also provide a way out so that you can stand up under it. Therefore, my dear friends, flee from idolatry. I speak to sensible people; judge for yourselves what I say" (1 Corinthians 10:13–15).

Be sensible and keep technology in its proper place and acknowledge God in His.

Significant Other

It seems to me that so much of what happens online is actually a search for personal significance. People mine the Internet like a vein of ore, looking for nuggets of value to barter for social cachet. People log on to Facebook to establish a connection to others, to friend as a verb, siphoning off self-esteem by the numbers. Cell phones act as a surrogate voice, crying "Look at me!" and "Pay attention to me!" in multiple digital languages. All of this is done in a cyber-environment that does little to encourage true intimacy, honesty, and authentic transparency.

As human beings, we desire connection. We were made that way by a God who exists within relationship Himself (Genesis 2:18; 1:26). Significance is a way for us to trade for relationship, for love, for connection. Our significance, our value, our worth, however, is not measured by the gadgets we own, our quantity of online friends, how often we're retweeted, or how quickly someone returns our texts. All of these things are a poor foundation for self-esteem. Wise people, Scripture tells us, are careful where they build their foundations for life; shaky foundations end up going "splat!" (See Matthew 7:24–26.)

The foundation of our sense of self, of our value and worth as a person, is best built on a true knowledge of who we are in the spiritual world, not the illusion we've crafted for ourselves in the cyber-world. The truly significant other in our lives should be our heavenly Father, not whomever we can friend on the Internet.

Our significance, our value, our worth, however, is not measured by the gadgets we own, our quantity of online friends, how often we're retweeted, or how quickly someone returns our texts.

God, through Scripture and through Jesus Christ, has shown His desire and plan to "friend" us for eternity; we are considered not only friends of Jesus (John 15:15) but also children of God (1 John 3:1). What other significance do we need? What profile, title, or descriptor could possibly top that? It is our own insecurity and lack of faith hindering our ability to accept and integrate the truth of our divine significance into our lives. When we doubt how eternally precious we are to God, we choose to substitute temporal significance, often found through the things we buy and the masks we create. God's love is a much stronger, long-lasting foundation. It is freely given and eternal (Ephesians 1:6; John 3:16); no upgrades are needed, ever.

DIFFICULT BIRTH

I remember writing about the Internet back in mid-1990s before cell phones and Facebook, before texting and tweeting. Many people were either indifferent to the "information superhighway" (as the World Wide Web was called back then), or they took a decidedly "don't tell me what to do" approach to this brand-new toy. I felt a little like the prophet Jeremiah. One area I sounded a warning bell on was Internet pornography, which constituted a huge bulk of the money being made on the Internet even then. A decade ago the main pornography portals were websites. Who could anticipate handheld computers and teenagers sexting pictures to each other between algebra and world history?

Today there are hundreds of millions of pornographic pages on the Internet generating billions of dollars in revenue worldwide. This isn't going away any time soon. The pornographic presence on the Internet is a reality that needs to be considered by anyone, at any age, using the Internet. It's a great big global neighborhood out there, with a substantial cesspool of filth. If you want to go online, you have to think about, prepare, and guard yourself against the presence of Internet pornography.

A decade ago the main pornography portals were websites. Who could anticipate handheld computers and teenagers sexting pictures to each other between algebra and world history?

It's remarkably easy to become snared in pornography, especially visual porn for men. We talked about this in chapter 6; the progression of inadvertent viewing to intentional usage can be as short as a single image. Where pornography is concerned, James 1:13–15 is very valuable:

> When tempted, no one should say, "God is tempting me." For God cannot be tempted by evil, nor does he tempt anyone; but each one is tempted when, by his own evil desire, he is dragged away and enticed. Then, after desire has conceived, it gives birth to sin; and sin, when it is full-grown, gives birth to death.

Pornography is graphic, powerful, and highly addicting because of its connection to physical sexual arousal and release.

Pornography's progression is not unlike that which happened to golfer Tiger Woods. A friend of mine recounted a conversation he had about Tiger. A group of guys were together bemoaning Tiger's fall from grace when my friend asked a perceptive question: "Do you know how all this got started in the first place?" In the silence that followed, he supplied the answer. "Tiger said yes one time."

All you need to do to become addicted to pornography is say yes one time. The first yes makes the second one easier. The second yes makes the third one inevitable.

Providing immediate access and easy use, the Internet and digital devices are highly dangerous. You will need to monitor your own behavior and that of your family. Together you must keep each other accountable, and that means employing filters where appropriate and installing programs to track or block website usage where necessary. It may mean using a cell phone that can text but not receive pictures.

If you or a family member has a problem with Internet pornography, you need to seek professional help immediately. The addiction is progressive and its grip compellingly strong, requiring knowledgeable strategies to overthrow.

CONTROL ISSUE

Technology taps into our inner two-year-old, that part of our personality that grasps tightly to our toys and screams "Mine!" at the top of our lungs. It's fun and popular and necessary; we *need* it. It helps us to be in charge and dependent upon no one but ourselves (and, occasionally, the tech guy on the other end of the phone).

With technology we decide what we want to do, where we want to go, whom we access, and who accesses us. Some pieces of technology may come with a controller, but every piece of technology is, itself, a controller. It controls some part of our world and gives us access to that power.

The first yes makes the second one easier. The second yes makes the third one inevitable.

Technology also satisfies our need for instant gratification, a trait we picked up as toddlers and have tenaciously held on to. The concept of waiting is a difficult one for many of us, and technology hasn't helped. We have the digital attention span of a virtual fruit fly, skimming our Internet hits in staccato bursts, looking for the next juicy morsel to land on. This mile-wide, inch-thick digital landscape can easily become the new normal. When something doesn't work quite right or as quickly as it should, the interruption in that stream of control inspires feelings of irritation and frustration, impatience and entitlement. Irritation, frustration, impatience, and entitlement are not spiritual virtues; they are the polar opposites of love, joy, peace, patience, kindness, goodness, faithfulness, gentleness, and self-control—the fruit of the Spirit described in Galatians 5:22–23.

We are impatient, shortsighted people, and Scripture is quite clear that our ways are not God's ways (Isaiah 55:8). Our timing isn't exactly divine, either: "Do not let this one fact escape your notice, beloved, that with the Lord a day is like a thousand years, and a thousand years like a day" (2 Peter 3:8, NAS). Granted, waiting a day for your Internet to get fixed can *seem* like a thousand years, but it's not. We get incensed when it takes twenty seconds to load a webpage. In contrast, God's purposes and plans can take millennia to develop and come to fulfillment. So, from our perspective, it seems that God is dragging His feet, especially when we deeply want something. The apostle Peter goes on to say, "The Lord is not slow in keeping his promise, as some understand slowness. He is patient with you, not wanting anyone to perish, but everyone to come to repentance" (2 Peter 3:9). God's view is a decidedly long view. In God's lexicon, *slow* is not a dirty word.

We need to stop and consider consequences, and we need to stop and take a deep breath. We need to stop and evaluate how fast-paced our lives have become and the resultant levels of dissatisfaction and stress we embrace because of it. The more exposure you have to technology, the shorter your view can become, so you need to be alert to increased levels of frustration and impatience not only with the devices you use but also with the people you come in contact with. Frequent technology use shortens fuses, so you need to be on your guard.

Watchers

You need to be on your guard, watching what you do, because you're not the only one watching. There are others around you watching too. They are your family members and loved ones, your coworkers and acquaintances. They are those who know Jesus and those who don't. We can become so absorbed with the technology we use that we forget other people can see us. They see us and make value judgments about what we say as opposed to what we do and how we live our lives.

You and I have influence over the watchers in our lives. Some of those watchers will be fellow adults, able to utilize mature life experience to interpret what they see. Some of those watchers will be children, who don't yet have the perspective and experience to interpret an adult world. Where technology is concerned, you can bet those younger watchers will be paying close attention; after all, this is their turf. In some ways the kids of today think of technology as their birthright. Like the prodigal son, some of them want the control of it right now. You need to provide a loving, adult example of how to *improve* life with technology, not surrender to it.

We can become so absorbed with the technology we use that we forget other people can see us.

Shiny New Toy

I've used the analogy before of technology being like a shiny new toy. I'd like to use it again for one more analogy: shiny things have a way of acting like a mirror, showing you a reflection of yourself. If I am honest with myself, I have to admit I haven't always liked the person peering back at me from the devices I've used. They have sometimes shown me a person much more self-absorbed and self-consumed than I want to admit. Going through this book has caused me to cringe more than once at the "me" I've seen reflected in my technology use.

The truth is hard to admit but good to recognize. That's how growth happens. None of us are perfect, and we are constantly presented with the opportunity to learn from our mistakes and take advantage of the chance to change our lives for the better. I know that's what I'm going to do with what I've learned through this experience; I pray that's what you're going to do, and I think God's rooting for it too. This book has been an opportunity for you to come face-to-face with some truths that may be difficult to accept. The truth, however, is not meant to overwhelm and discourage you but to motivate you to grow and mature, one step, one truth, one day at a time.

So, don't be consumed with guilt over what you've learned. Instead, be empowered to change. Lamentations 3:22–23 reminds each of us that, "Because of the LORD's great love we are not consumed, for his compassions never fail. They are new every morning; great is your faithfulness." I may have stumbled today, but I trust God to help pick me up and set me back on my feet tomorrow. I believe God is more powerful than any technology created by man's hand, and He is able to guide me where technology is concerned. With His help I am able to control my use of technology for good.

CONNECTION SECTION

For this final exercise I'd like you to make a vow to the Lord. I recognize that seems like an old-fashioned notion to use in a book about technology. However, we still use vows in this culture—marriage vows, for example. A vow is a pledge, a promise to be bound by your word. I'd like you to make a vow to the Lord about your use of technology from this day forward. I offer mine as an example for you to take as your own, if you choose, or as an illustration for one you will craft for yourself. Yes, the following vow is short, but I intend to memorize it so it can easily come to mind when I'm frustrated and distracted and tempted to give in.

> *Lord, I give my use of technology over to You. I will have no other gods before You, including a digital one.*

I pledge to be thoughtful in what I use, prudent in how I use it, and mindful of the power it has claimed in my life. I vow to place no digital god above You in my life.

Thank you for taking this journey with me. You can find me on Facebook and Twitter. I also have a couple of websites where you can find out about me (DrGregoryJantz.com) or my counseling center (APlaceOfHope.com).

A vow is a pledge, a promise to be bound by your word.

May each of us grab hold of Colossians 3:17: "And whatever you do, whether in word or deed, do it all in the name of the Lord Jesus, giving thanks to God the Father through him." May God be pleased by all we do in our lives—online and off.

NOTES

INTRODUCTION
THIS IS THE AIR I BREATHE

1. Maia Szalavitz, "Steve Jobs Had LSD. We Have the iPhone," *Healthland*, Time.com, October 6, 2011, http://healthland.time .com/2011/10/06/jobs-had-lsd-we-have-the-iphone/ (accessed December 7, 2011).
2. Phil LeBeau, "Texting and Driving Worse Than Drinking and Driving," CNBC.com, June 25, 2009, http://www.cnbc.com/ id/31545004/site/14081545/ (accessed December 7, 2011).
3. Figures in chart taken from Florida Museum of Natural History, "Annual Risk of Death During One's Lifetime," http:// www.flmnh.ufl.edu/fish/sharks/attacks/relarisklifetime.html (accessed December 7, 2011).

CHAPTER 1
A LOCKED FRONT DOOR AND A WIDE OPEN WEB

1. Alex Trimpe, "The World Is Obsessed With Facebook," YouTube.com, uploaded February 21, 2011, http://www

.youtube.com/watch?v=xJXOavGwAW8&noredirect=1 (accessed November 29, 2011).

2. Emma Barnett, "Google+ Isn't a Social Network: It's a Web Spider Hungry for Your Data," *The Telegraph*, November 11, 2011, http://www.telegraph.co.uk/technology/google/8883449/Google-isnt-a-social-network-its-a-web-spider-hungry-for-your-data.html (accessed December 7, 2011).

3. SocialWay, "20 Social Media Statistics," posted November 16, 2011, https://www.facebook.com/notes/socialway/20-social-media-statistics/ 301647373193264 (accessed November 29, 2011).

4. Facebook, "Statistics," https://www.facebook.com/press/info.php?statistics (accessed November 29, 2011).

5. Actually, 1,330,928 years: (700 billion minutes) / (1 year) = 1,330,928.11 years.

6. Facebook, "Statistics" (accessed November 29, 2011).

7. Associated Press, "Craigslist Killing Trial Goes to Jury in Tacoma," *Seattle Times*, March 8, 2011, http://seattletimes.nwsource.com/html/localnews/2014433754_apwacraigslist-killing.html (accessed November 29, 2011). Also, Christine Clarridge, "Fourth Suspect in Fatal Home-Invasion Surrenders," *Seattle Times*, May 7, 2010, http://seattletimes.nwsource.com/html/localnews/2011800584_homeinvasion07m.html (accessed November 29, 2011).

8. Claudia Buck, "Internet Swindlers Grow More Sophisticated," *Seattle Times*, February 26, 2011, http://seattletimes.nwsource.com/html/businesstechnology/2014294766_pfwebscams27.html (accessed November 29, 2011).

9. Bruce Schreiner and Janet Cappiello Blake (AP), "Soldier Impersonators Target Women in Web Scams," ABCNews.com, February 27, 2011, http://abcnews.go.com/US/wireStory?id=13012722 (accessed November 29, 2011).

10. Kim Zetter, "Prosecutors Drop Plans to Appeal Lori Drew Case," Wired.com, November 20, 2009, http://www.wired.com/threatlevel/2009/11/lori-drew-appeal (accessed November 29, 2011).

11. *Agence France-Presse*, "Internet Is World's 'Greatest Spying Machine': Assange," Inquirer.net, March 16, 2011, http://newsinfo.inquirer.net/breakingnews/infotech/view/20110316 -325729/Internet-is-worlds-greatest-spying-machineAssange (accessed November 29, 2011).

12. Byron Acohido, "Facebook Tracking Is Under Scrutiny," USAToday.com, November 16, 2011, http://www.usatoday .com/tech/news/story/2011-11-15/facebook-privacy-tracking -data/51225112/1?csp=34money (accessed December 7, 2011).

13. University of Utah News Center, "Drivers on Cell Phones Are as Bad as Drunks," June 29, 2006, http://unews.utah.edu/old/ p/062206-1.html (accessed November 29, 2011).

CHAPTER 2
MULTI-TAXED

1. CBSNews.com, "Texting While Walking, Woman Falls Into Fountain," January 20, 2011, http://www.cbsnews.com/stories/2011/ 01/20/earlyshow/main7265096.shtml (accessed November 29, 2011).

2. Linda Stone, "Q&A: Continuous Partial Attention," LindaStone .net, http://lindastone.net/qa/ (accessed November 29, 2011).

3. Annie Burris, "Man Who Killed Bicyclist Gets 6 Years," *Orange County Register*, December 29, 2009, http://www.ocregister .com/articles/woods-223842-maximum-oates.html (accessed December 7, 2011).

4. EloM-Msa Ruano GonzM-Alez, "Victim's Family Seeks Ban on Texting While Driving," *Orlando Sentinel*, February 13, 2009, http://articles.orlandosentinel.com/2009-02-13/news/ texting13_1_cell-heather-hurd-phones (accessed December 7, 2011).

5. Associated Press, "Feds Probe Texting Before Deadly Train Crash," MSNBC.com, September 15, 2008, http://www.msnbc .msn.com/id/26718585/ (accessed December 7, 2011).

6. Michele McPhee, "Texting Trolley Driver Could Face Charges," ABCNews.com, May 11, 2009, http://abcnews.go.com/US/ story?id=7561561&page=1 (accessed December 7, 2011).

7. *Good Morning America*, "Are We a Nation of 'Pseudo-ADD' Sufferers?," June 13, 2005, http://abcnews.go.com/GMA/OnCall/story?id=842263&page=1 (accessed November 29, 2011).

8. Matt Richtel, "Drivers and Legislators Dismiss Cellphone Risks," *New York Times*, July 18, 2009, http://www.nytimes.com/2009/07/19/technology/19distracted.html (accessed November 29, 2011).

9. Eyal Ophir, Clifford Nass, and Anthony D. Wagner, "Cognitive Control in Media Multitaskers," *Proceedings of the National Academy of Sciences* (August 24, 2009): http://www.pnas.org/content/early/2009/08/21/0903620106.abstract (accessed November 29, 2011).

10. Sharon Begley, "I Can't Think!", *Newsweek*, February 27, 2011, http://www.thedailybeast.com/newsweek/2011/02/27/i-can-t-think.html (accessed November 29, 2011).

11. *Newsweek*, March 7, 2011, cover, viewed at http://www.amazon.com/NEWSWEEK-Magazine-2011-Brain-Freeze/dp/B004QIWCUI (accessed November 29, 2011).

12. *The Economist*, "The Tyranny of Choice: You Choose," December 16, 2010, http://www.economist.com/node/17723028 (accessed November 29, 2011).

13. BrainyQuote.com, "Abraham Lincoln Quotes," http://www.brainyquote.com/quotes/quotes/a/abrahamlin109275.html (accessed November 29, 2011).

14. Claudia Wallis, "genM: The Multitasking Generation," *Time*, March 27, 2006, http://www.time.com/time/magazine/article/0,9171,1174696,00.html (accessed December 7, 2011).

Chapter 3
This Is Your Brain on YouTube

1. Dalton Conley, "Wired for Distraction: Kids and Social Media," *Time*, March 19, 2011, http://www.time.com/time/magazine/article/0,9171,2048363,00.html (accessed November 29, 2011).

2. Wikipedia.org, s.v. "List of Internet Phenomena," http://en.wikipedia.org/wiki/List_of_Internet_phenomena (accessed December 7, 2011).

3. Wikipedia.org, s.v. "Delayed Gratification," http://en.wikipedia .org/wiki/Delayed_gratification (accessed December 7, 2011).

Chapter 4
Thank You for Being a Friend

1. Merriam-Webster, *Merriam-Webster's Collegiate Dictionary*, 11th ed. (Springfield, MA: Merriam-Webster, Inc., 2003), s.v. "friend."

2. ThinkExist.com, "Aristotle Quotes," http://thinkexist.com/ quotation/what_is_a_friend-a_single_soul_dwelling_in_ two/12811.html (accessed November 30, 2011).

3. ThinkExist.com, "Walter Winchell Quotes," http://thinkexist .com/quotation/a_real_friend_is_one_who_walks_in_when_ the_rest/15163.html (accessed November 30, 2011).

4. ThinkExist.com, "Oscar Wilde Quotes," http://thinkexist .com/quotation/a_true_friend_stabs_you_in_the_front/217428 .html (accessed November 30, 2011).

5. QuoteWorld.org, "Friends," http://quoteworld.org/categories/ friends/9/ (accessed November 30, 2011).

6. BrainyQuote.com, "Friendship Quotes," http://www .brainyquote.com/quotes/topics/topic_friendship.html (accessed November 30, 2011).

7. ThinkExist.com, "Robert Brault Quotes," http://thinkexist .com/quotation/i_value_the_friend_who_for_me_finds_time_ on_his/224525.html (accessed November 30, 2011).

8. BrainyQuote.com, "Oprah Winfrey Quotes," http://www .brainyquote.com/quotes/quotes/o/oprahwinfr105255.html (accessed November 30, 2011).

9. Proverbs 27:6, NIV.

10. Facebook, "Statistics" (accessed November 30, 2011).

11. Carl Bialik, "Sorry, You May Have Gone Over Your Limit of Network Friends," *Wall Street Journal*, November 16, 2007, http://online.wsj.com/article/SB119518271549595364.html (accessed November 30, 2011).

12. Charles Cooper, "How I Nearly Got Scammed on Facebook," CBSNews.com, April 5, 2011, http://www.cbsnews

.com/8301-501465_162-20051016-501465.html (accessed November 30, 2011).

13. Geoffrey Fowler, "Jimmy Kimmel's 'Unfriend Day' Is a Hot Start-Up Idea," *Digits* (blog), *Wall Street Journal*, November 17, 2010, http://blogs.wsj.com/digits/2010/11/17/jimmy-kimmels-unfriend-day-is-a-hot-start-up-idea/ (accessed November 30, 2011).

14. Angus Stevenson, "A Century of Defining Our Language," *Oxford Words* (blog), August 18, 2011, http://blog.oxforddictionaries.com/2011/08/century-defining-language/ (accessed December 7, 2011).

CHAPTER 5
JUST LIKE REAL LIFE

1. Merriam-Webster, *Merriam-Webster's Collegiate Dictionary*, s.v. "virtual."

2. Hiroko Tabuchi, "Facebook Wins Relatively Few Friends in Japan," *New York Times*, January 9, 2011, http://www.nytimes.com/2011/01/10/technology/10facebook.html?_r=1 (accessed November 30, 2011).

3. EbizMBA.com, "Top 15 Most Popular Social Networking Sites," December 5, 2011, ebizmba.com/articles/social-networking-websites (accessed December 7, 2011).

4. Erik Davis, *TechGnosis: Myth, Magic and Mysticism in the Age of Information* (n.p.: Five Star, 2005), 190.

5. William Shakespeare, *As You Like It* 2.7, http://shakespeare.mit.edu/asyoulikeit/full.html (accessed November 30, 2011). Numbers refer to act and scene.

6. Chris Matyszczyk, "Teen Denies Crime, but Admits It on Facebook," CNET.com, April 23, 2011, http://news.cnet.com/8301-17852_3-20056693-71.html (accessed November 30, 2011).

CHAPTER 6
REAL CONNECTION

1. Find more stories at http://stories.twitter.com/.

2. Consumer-Rankings.com, "The Best 5 Dating Sites of 2011," December 1, 2011, http://www.consumer-rankings.com/dating/ (accessed December 2, 2011).

3. Consumer-Rankings.com, "Match.com," http://www.consumer-rankings.com/dating/matchreview (accessed December 2, 2011).

4. Consumer-Rankings.com, "Chemistry.com," http://www.consumer-rankings.com/dating/chemistryreview (accessed December 2, 2011).

5. Consumer-Rankings.com, "PerfectMatch," http://www.consumer-rankings.com/dating/perfectmatchreview (accessed December 2, 2011).

6. Consumer-Rankings.com, "eHarmony," http://www.consumer-rankings.com/dating/eharmonyreview (accessed December 2, 2011).

7. Consumer-Rankings.com, "Spark.com," http://www.consumer-rankings.com/dating/sparkreview (accessed December 2, 2011).

8. Kim Linton, "Penthouse Media Launches Christian Dating Site: BigChurch.com," Yahoo! Voices, May 22, 2008, http://voices.yahoo.com/penthouse-media-launches-christian-dating-site-bigchurchcom-1470341.html (accessed December 2, 2011). Techwhack.com, "Penthouse Media Group to Enter Social Networking Market," December 13, 2007, http://business.techwhack.com/3334-penthouse-media-group/ (accessed December 2, 2011).

9. Desmond Morris, *Intimate Behavior: A Zoologist's Classic Study of Human Intimacy* (New York: Kodansha Globe, 1997), 74–78.

10. Ibid.

11. Rachel B. Duke, "More Women Lured to Pornography Addiction," *Washington Times*, July 11, 2010, http://www.washingtontimes.com/news/2010/jul/11/more-women-lured-to-pornography-addiction/?page=all (accessed December 2, 2011).

12. Ryan Singel, "Internet Porn: Worse Than Crack?," Wired.com, November 19, 2004, http://www.wired.com/science/discoveries/news/2004/11/65772 (accessed December 2, 2011).

13. OnlineMBA.com, "The Stats on Internet Porn," *Infographics* (blog), June 18, 2010, http://www.onlinemba.com/blog/the-stats -on-internet-porn/ (accessed December 2, 2011).

14. Merriam-Webster, *Merriam-Webster's Collegiate Dictionary*, s.v. "pornography."

15. Max Frisch, *Homo Faber*, trans. Michael Bullock (Orlando, FL: Houghton Mifflin Harcourt, 1959), 178.

CHAPTER 7
INSTANT DOWNLOAD

1. Wikipedia.org, s.v. "Moore's Law," http://en.wikipedia.org/wiki/ Moore%27s_law (accessed December 7, 2011).

2. Patrick Morley, *Seven Seasons of the Man in the Mirror* (Grand Rapids, MI: Zondervan, 1997), 137.

3. Elyse Kaner, "Writer's Block: Electronic Phonics," ABCNewspapers.com, November 2, 2011, http://abcnewspapers .com/2011/11/02/writers-block-electronic-phonics/ (accessed December 7, 2011).

CHAPTER 8
THE ANGST OF OFF-LINE

1. Greg Lamm, "UW Researchers Focus on Wearable Computers for Your Eyeballs," TechFlash.com, November 22, 2011, http:// techflash.com/seattle/2011/11/uw-researchers-and-wearable -computers.html (accessed December 7, 2011).

2. Solutions Research Group, "Age of Disconnect Anxiety and Four Reasons Why It's Difficult to Stay Off the Grid," US Research Summary, March 2008, http://srgnet.com/pdf/ disconnect_anxiety_us_summary_mar08.pdf (accessed December 2, 2011).

3. Michelle Hackman, "Communication Underload: Validating the Existence of Disconnect Anxiety," John. L. Miller Great Neck North High School, http://people.hofstra.edu/ Vincent_R_Brown/Hackman_CommunicationUnderload.pdf (accessed December 2, 2011).

4. *Great Neck Record*, "Intel Winner Michelle Hackman," March 25, 2011, http://www.antonnews.com/greatneckrecord/ news/14265-intel-winner-michelle-hackman.html (accessed December 2, 2011).

5. Helen Leggatt, "53% of Youngsters Would Give Up Sense of Smell to Stay Connected," BizReport.com, May 26, 2011, http:// www.bizreport.com/2011/05/53-of-youngsters-would-give-up -sense-of-smell-to-stay-connec.html# (accessed December 2, 2011).

6. "Going 24 Hours Without Media," *the world UNPLUGGED* (blog), http://theworldunplugged.wordpress.com/ (accessed December 2, 2011).

7. Ibid.

8. Plato, *Phaedrus*, trans. Benjamin Jowett, Philosophy.eserver .org, http://philosophy.eserver.org/plato/phaedrus.txt (accessed December 7, 2011).

9. "Going 24 Hours Without Media."

10. Jessica Dickler, "$67 Billion in Vacation Days, Out the Window," CNNMoney, May 25, 2011, http://money.cnn.com/2011/05/25/pf/ unused_vacation_days/index.htm (accessed December 5, 2011).

11. YouTube.com, "AT&T Commercial: Funny Email," http://www .youtube.com/watch?v=hwZWJWmOzeg (accessed December 5, 2011).

CHAPTER 9
TRANSFER OF POWER

1. Jessica Guynn, "Survey: Parents Lie to Help Preteens Get on Facebook," *Technology* (blog), *Los Angeles Times*, November 2, 2011, http://latimesblogs.latimes.com/technology/2011/11/ survey-parents-lie-to-help-preteens-get-on-facebook.html (accessed December 7, 2011).

2. Liz Perle, "The Side Effects of Media," CommonsenseMedia .org, January 20, 2010, http://www.commonsensemedia.org/ advice-for-parents/side-effects-media (accessed December 5, 2011).

3. Barna Group, *The Family and Technology Report: How Technology Is Helping Families—and Where They Need Help*, State of the Church and Family, 2011 Annual Report. Available from Barna.org.

4. Amanda Lenhart, Rich Ling, Scott Campbell, and Kristen Purcell, "Teens and Mobile Phones," Pew Internet and American Life Project, April 20, 2010, http://pewinternet.org/Reports/2010/Teens-and-Mobile-Phones.aspx (accessed December 5, 2011).

5. Matt Richtel, "E-Mail Gets an Instant Makeover," *New York Times*, December 20, 2010, http://www.nytimes.com/2010/12/21/technology/21email.html (accessed December 5, 2011).

6. Diana Hefley, "Topless Photos Exposed, Lynnwood Police Say," HeraldNet.com, June 14, 2011, http://www.heraldnet.com/article/20110614/NEWS01/706149906 (accessed December 5, 2011).

7. Ibid.

8. Barna Group, *The Family and Technology Report: How Technology Is Helping Families—and Where They Need Help*.

CHAPTER 10
WHO ARE YOU, REALLY?

1. Richard Waters, "Identity and the Internet: From Pixels to Persona," *Financial Times*, November 21, 2011, http://www.ft.com/intl/cms/s/0/0585597c-1435-11e1-85c7-00144feabdc0.html#axzz1fwz7vZWB (accessed December 8, 2011).

2. Arthur C. Clarke, *Profiles of the Future* (n.p.: V. Gollancz, 1962).

CHAPTER 11
FIND THE OFF SWITCH

1. Danielle Dellorto, "WHO: Cell Phone Use Can Increase Possible Cancer Risk," CNN.com, May 31, 2011, http://www.cnn.com/2011/HEALTH/05/31/who.cell.phones/index.html (accessed December 6, 2011).

2. Andrew Weil, "Why 'Data Smog' May Be Making You Depressed," *Time*, November 14, 2011, http://ideas.time .com/2011/11/14/why-data-smog-may-be-making-you-depressed/ (accessed December 8, 2011).

3. Frisch, *Homo Faber*, 178.

CHAPTER 12
THE ULTIMATE FILTER

1. Neil Postman, *The End of Education: Redefining the Value of School* (New York: Alfred A. Knopf, 1995), 38.

The Secret *to* True Happiness!

Gregory Jantz provides a
[roa]d map to true happiness that
[isn']t based on past, present,
[or] future circumstances or
[exp]eriences. Discover…

[F]OUR STEPS TO
CONTENTMENT, HOPE,
[A]ND JOY

[T]HREE KEYS TO STAYING
[H]APPY

[T]HREE DETOURS YOU
MUST AVOID!

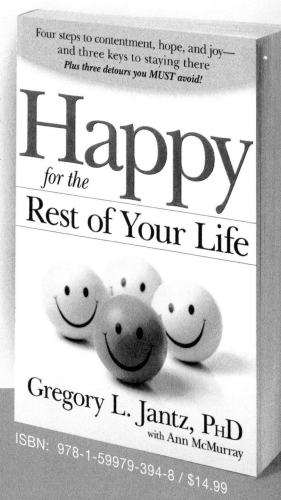

Four steps to contentment, hope, and joy—
and three keys to staying there
Plus three detours you MUST avoid!

Happy
for the
Rest of Your Life

Gregory L. Jantz, PhD
with Ann McMurray

ISBN: 978-1-59979-394-8 / $14.99

[A]vailable where fine
[C]hristian books are sold
[Find] us: Facebook.com/CharismaHouse

SILOAM

10683

FREE NEWSLETTERS
TO HELP EMPOWER YOUR LIFE

Why subscribe today?

- ☐ **DELIVERED DIRECTLY TO YOU.** All you have to do is open your inbox and read.

- ☐ **EXCLUSIVE CONTENT.** We cover the news overlooked by the mainstream press.

- ☐ **STAY CURRENT.** Find the latest court rulings, revivals, and cultural trends.

- ☐ **UPDATE OTHERS.** Easy to forward to friends and family with the click of your mouse.

CHOOSE THE E-NEWSLETTER THAT INTERESTS YOU MOST:

- Christian news
- Daily devotionals
- Spiritual empowerment
- And much, much more

SIGN UP AT: **http://freenewsletters.charismamag.com**

#178